15⁰⁰

INTRODUCTION TO
MOUNTAINEERING

Ad Astra Per Aspera

George Alan Smith

INTRODUCTION TO
MOUNTAINEERING

*No mountaineer who respects common sense
and mistrusts sentimentality will claim
for mountain-climbing that it is more,
primarily, than a great sport — if perhaps
the greatest. It is a high enough claim.*

GEOFFREY WINTHROP YOUNG

INTRODUCTION BY JAMES RAMSEY ULLMAN

A. S. Barnes and Company · New York

To
Lois

Foreword

*Our competition with the mountain injures
no other human competitor by our success.
Our conquest of them ends only in the conquest of ourselves.*

GEOFFREY WINTHROP YOUNG

A GRIZZLED CRAGSMAN, seeing a young friend poring over a manual
of climbing technique, exclaimed, "Hrmph! You don't expect to learn
to climb from a book, do you?" Taken aback, the young man did not
answer at once, so a discussion did not ensue. Yet the conversation
need not have ended so abruptly; there was material for talk and it
might have taken the tack that theory and practice go hand in hand.
Nobody would aver, of course, that an armchair mountaineer can be
anything but just that, whereas with competent instruction, constant
practice and sufficient experience anyone with a taste for the hills may
become an adequate climber.

Competent instruction, however, is not always available. A fine
mountaineer may not of necessity be a good teacher, although for the
observant novice there is nothing better than going behind a skillful
climber. Actually, the lad with the manual was on the right track.
Browsing through his book, reading how others had solved technical
problems, he was preparing himself to climb better. He was assuming
that he still had much to learn, a healthy attitude to maintain in a
sport where even experts admit that mountains always have surprises
in store.

The wise novice will adopt a middle path: he will not assume
that a climbing book per se provides an open sesame to the high hills;
he will not eschew information which books about the sport may
impart. The fact is, one must learn to climb as one can, when one can

and where one can. Given a natural flair, progress may be rapid, perhaps too rapid for one's own good. In climbing, it is frequently the case of the tortoise and the hare: slow and steady gets there first. It may well be costly to emulate the hare on a mountainside. He who is content to grow slowly as a mountaineer will inevitably have a longer career.

That climbing is not exclusively a physical pastime is not always understood by the groundling. This is reflected by the difficulty of satisfactorily answering the non-believer's eternal "Why?" The dimensions of mountaineering are large, embracing something of man's craving for adventure, something of his desire to explore his world. It is a commonplace that George Leigh Mallory, the brilliant young Britisher who disappeared high on Mount Everest in 1924, answered the query "Why do you climb a mountain?" by saying "Because it is there!" No climber needs a better answer; perhaps no non-climber ever completely understands.

Mountaineers have been criticized for allowing this somewhat mystical aura to surround their sport. The aura is there despite the climber, not because he created it. If in the act of climbing a mountain a man finds spiritual satisfaction, such an experience inevitably informs his life. The intangibles of faith and belief are private affairs. If this cannot be explained to the satisfaction of the non-climber, it is a pity, yet nobody's fault.

The purpose of this book is to inculcate some of the fundamental principles of mountaineering, to convey some sense of the enormous satisfactions of the sport, into the minds and hearts of those who aspire to the heights. The ascent from the valley to the ramparts of the mountain, the struggle up rock-ribbed regions of snow and ice to the summit, the ensuing return to the valley, can take on the stature of something more than mere sport. It can become a way of life.

But it is only by achieving fine physical condition, by learning slowly and practicing carefully the technics of each branch of the sport until they become second nature, by learning to regard mountains with wholesome respect, that the climber can become the complete mountaineer.

George Alan Smith

Acknowledgments

ALL BOOKS are collaborations, and none more so than a book on mountaineering, a sport whose essence is cooperation. This book could not have been written, for instance, without a wife whose placid faith and trust have welcomed every return from the hills nor without parents whose confidence was always unbounded. Nor would it have come to pass without the many happy climbing days with Roger Wolcott, surely the best of all comrades on the rope.

I am also enormously beholden to the rock climbers of the New York Chapter of the Appalachian Mountain Club whose enthusiasm and skill is second to none and who have so patiently trained so many into proficiency. And there is especially Maria Leiper Millar, editor and agile climber, whose encouragement and advice have been freely offered both on and off the rocks.

For direct assistance, and for permission to use photographs, I must thank the Swiss National Travel Office, especially its ebullient Dr. Max Senger at Zurich who gave unstinted help. For their generous permission to use photographs of them in this book, thanks also to Swiss guides Leo Summermatter of Randa and Siegfried Bumann of Saas Fee. And gratitude to Sidney Nowill, author of *The Mountains of My Life,* for permission to use his fine picture of the Südlenz-Nadelgrat ridge.

Acknowledgment is also due photographers Leslie Gill and Duncan Edwards for permitting use of their composite photograph which appears on the dust jacket, and to Ogilvy Benson & Mather for releasing the picture. Too, thanks must go to the Focal Press, London, for allowing use of a quotation from C. Douglas Milner's *Mountain Photography,* and to Methuen & Co. Ltd., London, for letting me quote from Geoffrey Winthrop Young's *Mountain Craft* and *On High Hills.* Kind assistance was also rendered by Miss Helene Fleck, assistant secretary of the American Alpine Club. And also a nod to·Hal Holbrook for reasons best known to himself.

To Delphine Wilde, and again to the indefatigable Roger, my warmest thanks for their patient travail in helping with the photography, and for their willingness to pore critically through the manuscript in the rough.

G. A. S.

Contents

Introduction

A FEW PAGES back, in his own foreword, George Alan Smith makes mention of one of the most formidable occupational hazards of the mountaineer: the struggle to answer satisfactorily the non-climber's eternal *"Why?"* For a good many years, both in talk and print, I myself have waged the battle with dubious success. But from here on, I think, the going will be easier. I shall simply distribute copies of *Introduction to Mountaineering,* with a sigh of thanks to Mr. Smith, and the conviction that if *it* doesn't bring light to the heathen, the heathen is beyond help.

For this book, it seems to me, achieves, with simplicity and clarity, precisely what it sets out to do, and I cannot imagine anyone who reads it ever again truthfully saying, "I know nothing about mountains." Do not let my first paragraph mislead you. Mr. Smith has written no philosophical treatise, nor has he an argumentative ax, ice- or otherwise, to grind. He is simply a man who knows and loves mountains (the two, I have always observed, are synonymous) and who here, as author, freely shares that knowledge and love with the uninitiated.

Most of his book is factual and practical: a discussion of how and — equally important — how not to climb. And the text is well abetted by vivid and instructive photographs. But again, do not be misled: it is not a treatise or a technical manual. Such books exist, and are highly useful in their specialized fields. But this one is not for specialists. It is for the curious asker of the eternal *"Why?"* And of the general *"How?"* And if its pages will not boost the reader to the top of Everest, or even up the crags of the nearest hilltop, it will, I guarantee, give him a sure and true insight into what mountaineering is all about.

It is, he will find, "about" many things. About rock and snow and ice. About wind and weather. About cliffs and ridges and gullies and glaciers; ropes and axes and pitons and belays; routes and route-finding and leadership and teamwork and safety and danger and success and disaster. All these aspects, and many more, Mr. Smith discusses in the pages that follow. And through it all — most important of all — runs his deep "feel" of the mountains: the knowledge that answers the *How?* and the love that answers the *Why?*

"The dimensions of mountaineering are large," he says; and he is not speaking of the size of peaks but of human experience. Into this small book he has packed a great wealth of that experience, in a way that will make it intelligible and fascinating even to the most earth-bound of non-climbers. So much for an introduction to *Introduction*. Tie onto the rope now with Mr. Smith, and be assured that you are climbing with a sound guide and good companion.

JAMES RAMSEY ULLMAN

chapter 1

A Legend

Not vainly did the early Persian make
His altar the high places and the peak
Of earth-o'er gazing mountains.

LORD BYRON

ONCE THERE was a man who wanted to climb a mountain. He didn't know why and he didn't know how. He only knew that a compulsion surpassing his own understanding lifted his eyes to the hills. This man was the first mountaineer. History does not record the man's name nor is there a record of the peak he conquered. Although tales of derring-do in the high places of the earth can be traced back many centuries, there is no written account of this pioneer's accomplishment. Folklore, too, has left him anonymous.

Yet the first mountaineer lived. He saw his mountain, he dreamed of standing on its summit. It is most likely that he kept his aspiration a secret, for even today there are still parts of the world where people believe that demons inhabit mountain tops. It is only a matter of decades, indeed, since such superstitions prevailed in parts of Europe, and vestiges are occasionally evidenced today. The first mountaineer, then, centuries ago, must have believed this, too. Yet the yearning to scale his mountain overcame any fear of evil spirits.

Although we may only speculate on this man's first ascent, it is not hard to reconstruct his story. He must have been dismayed again and again by the obstacles he had to surmount and quite likely he was repeatedly repulsed before he finally prevailed. But because he had the essential spirit of the true mountaineer, he persisted.

On the day he began his climb he pushed very high to where he could rest within a day's striking distance of the top. At first it was just plain slogging uphill against the inexorable pull of gravity. As his

Blümlisalphorn, showing crevasses, bergschrund, hanging glacier. (Courtesy Swiss National Travel Office.)

foray took him ever higher, he was surprised when the rarefied atmosphere oppressed him and inhibited his movements. In time, however, he found that his body adjusted and that he could thoroughly enjoy the keenness of the thinner air. By nightfall he found a satisfactory place to bivouac and to contemplate the sun's last rays gilding the topmost snows, those snows on which he hoped soon to stand.

Realizing that for safety he must regain his camp by the following evening, he retired betimes to his crude outdoor bed. He arose before daylight and his breakfast in the frosty air must have been cold and dispiriting. In the dim light of pre-dawn he began to move upward, finding the rocky way painful in his inadequate footgear. As daylight came, he crunched out on the glacier, alert for crevasses. A dangerous place to be alone, a glacier, but luck was on his side.

He paused to look up. There, incredibly high above, was the summit, the sun burnishing its frozen crest. Surely his mountain couldn't be as high as all that! He had been climbing for hours and — but, yes, it was as high as all that.

Now the climb began in earnest. There was the bergschrund to cross, that ugly crevasse where the steep mountainside meets the glacier. Gingerly he edged across a snowbridge which, luckily, did not give way. Slowly he moved onward, fighting fatigue, overcoming fear of height, fear of demons, fear of the unknown. There were rocky pitches of incredible steepness to climb, precipitously exposed places where the least slip would have cost his life. There were tedious snowslopes to ascend, slopes that seemed endless, each rounded and promising hummock proving only the shoulder to another of the same.

Later came the treacherous ice pitches that put even the lower crags to shame. There it had always been possible to have a hand or foot securely placed on something. Here it was as if he walked only on faith — which may well have been the truth.

But the gods were smiling that day as they watched the sport of mountaineering born. In time the ice was crossed, the precipices were climbed, the ridges topped. It was step and strain and pull and sweat. As the hours passed his limbs wearied beyond all imagination. It was no longer a case of looking up and glorying in a view of the lofty snows. It was learning the lesson of the hills.

Suddenly, unbelievably, there was nowhere else to go. The snowy ridge up which he toiled simply leveled off into a small plateau and there was no more *up*. This was the summit! Despite all difficulties, despite all caution, despite all resistings of mind, flesh and spirit, he had striven with the mountain and won. Now this was his mountain in truth. He could not have put into words why he had come but deep within him he knew.

It must have been a remarkable moment for this first mountaineer. There were no demons here unless they were the demons of fear he had now subdued. There was the wind, yes, and there was the cold. There was an appalling abyss on one hand and a frightening snow slope on the other. There may even have been a lingering doubt about the return trip yet to come. But above and beyond all this there was a

The summit ridge. Südlenz-Nadelgrat of the Mischabel group, Switzerland. (Courtesy of Sidney Nowill.)

sense of accomplishment, an exhilaration of mental and physical well-being; there was an incomparable view, and even, perhaps, a sense of being neighbor to God. It was a quiet interlude of exaltation, beyond telling, beyond sharing. Although it was only a comparative moment out of a lifetime, for the first mountaineer it would last until the end of his days.

It would have been a fitting reward if this pioneer of the high places of the earth could have known the significance of the path he blazed. He headed an ever-growing column that has stretched down the years and bids fair to extend into the immeasurable future. It is an impressive array: climbers who have conquered the Alps, the mighty cordilleras of North and South America, and those who have penetrated the Himalayan vastness to the summit of Everest itself. It is a fine company the first mountaineer keeps, a company from all walks of life: scholars, laborers, clerics, artists, scientists, soldiers, farmers, urbanites. Yes, it would have been nice, if, as he stood on his mountain-top, this man might have perceived the significance of his achievement, have glimpsed the shining faces that were to follow.

But he didn't ask for more. He had seen his mountain, he had dreamed his dream, he had climbed and he had won. What more could he possibly want as he stood on top of the world? There was nowhere else to go.

Nowhere else to go? Oh, but there was! Down again . . .

chapter 2

A True Story

Now for our mountain sport; up to yon hill!
SHAKESPEARE

IF THE history of the first mountaineer sounds apocryphal to the uninitiated, it will not to the seasoned mountaineer, for the sport has not
changed in its essentials over the ages. New and better equipment
has been provided, the limits of the possible have been raised, but the
joust between man and mountain retains the same basics. The rules of
the game cannot change for they are dictated by the mountain, not
by man.

Listen to a true story.

A recent summer, a young New Yorker, vacation-bent, decided
he wanted to climb a mountain. Who can answer for the vagaries of
human desire? For no rational reason, with little background and
experience, with no technical knowledge whatsoever, this young man
determined to attempt northern California's symmetrical Mount Shasta,
an extinct volcano in the northernmost High Sierras. With such brash
lack of mountaineering know-how, it mattered little what mountain
he selected for his exploit; the moral would have remained the same.
Fortunately he chose a mountain that does not normally abound in
difficulty. Conditions on any mountain of 14,000 feet, however, can
quickly become perilous, and severe accidents on Mt. Shasta are not
unknown.

Without proper advice or knowledge of what was required, this
young man prepared for his expedition. In the matter of footgear, for
instance, he went to a well-known sporting shop for climbing boots.
The clerk offered him a nice pair direct from Austria. That sounded
convincing and he took them. It just happened that these perfectly
good Austrian boots were designed for rock climbing, not for the rigors

of trail, scree slope, ice and snow. But of this our hero was blissfully unaware until later when, high on Shasta, the boot's thin sole began to peel off.

Other necessities were gathered rapidly and at random. A rucksack, of course, and warm clothing. An ice-ax? He decided not since skiing friends had told him the normal route would be straightforward. A sleeping bag seemed important, and some cooking utensils. A compass? He didn't even think of it.

Rucksack, rope, crampons and ice-ax, mountaineering "musts." (Courtesy Swiss National Travel Office.)

San Francisco was reached quickly by air and our friend proceeded to Shasta City where he bought provisions. Before hitch-hiking to Sand Flats where his climb was to begin, one formality remained: to notify the forest rangers that he was going on the mountain. He had been forewarned that these were seasoned men, skilled in distinguishing the experienced outdoorsman from the duffer. With some trepidation, therefore, he informed the ranger's office of his plans. An incredible part of this tale is that he was accepted as a bona fide mountaineer, given the ranger's blessing and told to proceed. In fact, only one cautionary word was offered: "There are bears up there," said the ranger, "but don't be afraid of them. They don't bite!"

So shortly after the city's turmoil, trudging through the giant forest was a refreshing experience. As the trail steepened and he bent to the task, our hero was certain that this was precisely the vacation he needed. Nobody could reach him here, not even by telephone, and this pleasant condition would last until he came down.

Enthusiasm for the task makes the work light, so he quickly reached the Sierra Mountaineering Club's hut at 8,000 feet, a substantial stone edifice with accommodations for a good-sized party although he was the lone occupant. Dumping his gear in the cabin, he emerged to look around. He was just at timberline and saw not far off a huge slope of rocks and boulders up which he would have to scramble. Above this he glimpsed snowfields leading to a high ridge which was the route to the summit.

The day seemed too good to waste so he decided to climb a bit to familiarize himself with the route. He started off vigorously and within fifty paces nearly fell down. What was this? He hadn't stumbled, there was no snow or ice, the going was, in fact, very easy. Once more he started forward only to discover that he couldn't make headway. What could be the matter? It was easy to guess. In hardly more than a day he had come from sea level to an altitude of a mile and a half. The rapid transition had not given his body time to adjust to the thinner air. Quite suddenly and naturally he had been stricken with mountain sickness. He would have to become acclimatized.

It speaks well for him that he spent another two hours that afternoon struggling up the rocks he had seen from the hut. On a slope he could readily have climbed had he been in proper condition he was reduced to crawling on hands and knees. In those two hours he scarcely gained five hundred feet. He had learned a simple fact the hard way, a fact he would not forget. Unless you live at high altitude, time for acclimatization must be allowed when you reach the mountains.

That evening he made himself as comfortable as possible in the cabin and dug in for a siege of Shasta. Despite the day's exercise he slept uneasily. The door of the hut could not be fastened and each time it creaked to and fro he wondered if a bear was nosing its way in.

Another day, another lesson. Taking lunch for higher on the mountain, he made for the ridge thinking to scout the summit route. He was grateful as he toiled upward that the sky was slightly overcast, for even in the nippy air he perspired freely from his exertion. He had climbed for a couple of hours before he noticed that the weather was closing in. No longer was the ridge visible, and looking back he was dismayed to find that mist obscured the return route. Since the trail was only an illy defined path across the rocks there was serious doubt about being able to find the way back to the cabin safely. It was with questionable optimism, therefore, that he pushed higher, hoping the sun would burn through. It didn't, and he was finally forced to retreat. Now, for the first time, as he consulted his map, he thought of a compass.

The next few hours were nightmarish. Nobody cares to have night close in 10,000 feet up a strange mountain. By continuation of his extraordinary good fortune he finally found the cabin again — not by skill, not by instinct, not by experience — just by luck and too close to nightfall for comfort. Despite the bears, he slept better that night.

Next day he climbed to take photographs, not pushing for the summit. When he was rather high, however, he heard a considerable noise below him. Since he couldn't identify it or discover the source, he remained in ignorance until he was descending in the late afternoon. There had been a rock avalanche, a tremendous downpouring of stone. To his horror, he saw that it had completely obliterated part of the route he had climbed that morning.

Afterwards he confessed to considerable uneasiness and not much sleep that night. He dreamed of rock and snow and ice, the door creaked more than ever, the wind sighed around the cabin like the sniffing of animals, the aloneness became oppressive. Nevertheless he was bent on one more effort.

The next day was not good for climbing and on the day following, although the clouds rode high enough and the weather seemed promising, there had been a snowfall that hampered his efforts, particularly in his inadequate boots. Mountain sickness, fatigue, loneliness, lack of training, all contributed toward stopping him short of the high ridge. He never even caught a close glimpse of the top of Mt. Shasta. He determined to return to the valley the next day en route home.

The hike down through the tall timber was pleasant and he was glad he had come even though the mountain had not been receptive. Upon reaching the valley he learned that there had been a severe storm on parts of the mountain during his stay. Luckily, only the edges had affected him. As a storekeeper in Shasta City morosely quipped, "We didn't expect to see *you* again."

Flying back to New York he had ample time to ruminate on his unusual vacation. He had learned something about the mountains certainly, although most of his new knowledge but highlighted by contrast his vast area of ignorance about mountaineering. After all, people did this for fun, scaling mountains higher and tougher than Shasta, and returned refreshed, invigorated, in excellent physical condition. Why hadn't he?

"I *can* climb Mt. Shasta," he thought. Then came the shattering answer. "But I failed!"

Something had caught fire in this young man, something which hitherto had lain dormant yet which may have been the incentive that impelled him at last to go to the mountains. He had acquired some first principles, quickly and painlessly. Not everyone who goes high for the first time is that lucky. A number of well-meaning but careless people had abetted him in his folly by selling or lending him equipment, giving him maps, good wishes and an encouraging slap on the shoulder. But somebody should have given him fundamental advice, for there are manifold dangers in the mountains awaiting the uninitiated or the unwary.

Soon after reaching home he phoned a friend who belonged to an eastern climbing organization. Over lunch the tale was told, straightforwardly, without frills, just the essentials of what had been an unsuccessful mountain adventure. There was laughter about the bears, seriousness over the mishaps, advice for the mistakes.

There was also the beginning of wisdom as our young friend asked, "How can I learn to climb a mountain?"

chapter 3

The Three Elements

Taste your legs, sir; put them to motion.
SHAKESPEARE

MOUNTAINEERING COMPRISES three outdoor sports — hiking, rock climbing, climbing on ice and snow. These sports may also be pursued independently and as they are quite different in nature are usually mastered separately. Blended, they form the art of mountain climbing.

The degree of difficulty varies widely within each category. It may alter yet again with the individual climber since people differ in aptitude and ability. It is common, for example, to see climbers who are unhappy on steep ice do seemingly impossible rock pitches with ease, or to see a man who has to struggle with a moderate stretch of rock chop easily and securely up a treacherous ice slope.

Clearly the desideratum is to feel at home in all aspects of the sport. There are brilliant climbers who are comfortable anywhere on a mountain even under the most discouraging circumstances. The average climber, however, of some competence and a certain flair, will be aware of his weaknesses as well as his strengths and adjust his climbing accordingly. In other words, he will strike a balance that is within his means and capability. Of course the climber must have faith in himself, but to climb with overconfidence is to indulge in a luxury that may be taxed very highly indeed.

In a mountaineering sense, hiking is synonymous with trail climbing. (It should be understood that the word "climbing" applies to the descent as well as to the upward trek.) Although there may not be a well-marked trail to follow, any walking accomplished on a mountain without use of the hands will fall within the definition of hiking as intended here.

Easy rock

Walking upward continuously on the lower reaches of a mountain, the part that is usually referred to as the approach, can be as arduous and wearying as those stretches of technical difficulty in the upper regions. Higher, in fact, the concentration on the task in hand may be so strong that fatigue will be felt only after the supreme effort is over rather than at the time of maximum exertion.

In training for a climbing vacation it is wise to spend as much time as possible actually on the trail. The more rugged the path, the better the training. This will not help lowlanders get acclimatized, their Colorado brethren having the advantage in this respect, but it will limber the walking muscles and shorten the conditioning period once the mountains are reached.

In areas where there are no snow-capped peaks, such as the Eastern seaboard of the United States, rock climbing has become a highly specialized art. There are purists who claim for rock climbing that it stands supreme, but to intrude on that debate is risky. Cragsmen being known for their rugged individualism, it is well to concede the point, letting who will cherish his own superior knowledge and taste.

Carefully developed, facility in scaling formidable cliffs can become a thing of comparative ease, although climbs are made nowadays that verge on the impossible. Not only is there tremendous satisfaction in being able to move lightly and carefully up thin rock faces, or to cope successfully with forbidding overhangs, but just to watch a well-coördinated rock climber moving up the cliffs is to perceive a rhythm and polish that is the envy of the less adroit and that may well leave the non-climber with a sense of awe.

The devotees of rock climbing have increased so rapidly in recent years, particularly since World War II, and the sport continues to grow at such pace, that organized climbing clubs are hard-pressed to meet the demands made upon them for participation and training. Unlike skiing, in which any novice with a pair of skis and a snowy slope at hand can practice solo at his peril, rock climbing requires teamwork. This is one good reason why an introduction to mountaineering is often made by training on the rocks. The essential bond of all climbers is the rope and on a cliff the novice can soon catch the significance of its use. As compared to the larger framework of mountaineering, however, rock climbing is an important technique that remains subordinate to the principal objective, the scaling of peaks.

Those who chafe most at the purist's claim for rock climbing are the ones who maintain that the most exhilarating experience of all is contending with a mountain's ice and snow. There can be no doubt that crunching across a high snowfield, or chopping up a precipitous slope, snatching at the frisky air of the higher altitudes, is one of the sport's great rewards. This aspect of mountaineering, of course, can also be the most fatiguing as anyone can attest who has plodded wearily up a seemingly unending ridge or snowfield.

Facility in the techniques of ice and snow mountaineering is harder come by than some dexterity in rock climbing, and much more explicit knowledge of prevailing conditions is required. Desirable as familiarity with some basics of geology may be for the rock climber, it is not paramount that he acquaint himself with such lore. The mountaineer without some knowledge of glacier structure and action, however, the varying types of ice, and the perils of snow under less than favorable conditions, is flirting with a danger out of proportion to the pleasures of the sport.

Crossing a glacier

Acquisition of such knowledge is not easy. Glacier research is a tremendous topic as is the study of avalanches. Although study goes on continuously in these fields, even the experts are not prepared to give other than partial answers. Dismaying as this may be to a novice climber, there are ways of gleaning a working know-how. Experience perforce must come first, preferably that gained by climbing under well-organized circumstances, whether with a club, with a friend of ability and experience, or climbing behind a seasoned guide.

Book knowledge is available and should be sought. Constant reference can be made to the bulletins and journals published by mountaineering groups, many of which report regularly on the latest findings. Climbers who are active skiers will already have familiarized themselves to some extent with snow conditions, giving them the edge in this portion of their climbing education, although winter conditions vary considerably from those of summer.

Hiking — rock climbing — climbing on snow and ice — these are the three elements of mountaineering. Once their essentials are grasped and practiced, some glimmerings of the sport's pleasures and satisfactions will become evident. Provided the climber gets himself into top physical condition, and assuming that he has the opportunity to learn from experienced friends, or as part of a climbing club, the chance of his developing into a competent mountaineer is good. There should be willingness to learn, there ought to be humor and patience, and there must be stamina. Lack of any of these will impede progress.

Physical attributes can be attained through sheer doggedness but the intangible qualities of good companionship, a sense of the time to be silent and the time to talk, the time to be in deadly earnest and the time for laughter, these innate virtues are beyond price in the high hills. Sensitivity to their values may make the difference between being a valued member of a mountaineering party or one whose presence relays unpleasant or unhappy messages up or down the rope.

chapter 4

How It Grew

To look back is wont to cheer climbing men.
DANTE

WITH THE initial conquest of Everest a long period of man's aspirations reached a climax. It was inevitable that one day Hillary and Tenzing — or two other mountaineers — would stand on top of the world. Man's adventurous spirit may be denied again and again but his ambition survives centuries until his goals are ultimately achieved.

The problem of ascending Everest had occupied climbers' thoughts for a hundred years, ever since a day in 1852 when a man rushed into the Surveyor General's India office crying, "Sir, I have discovered the highest mountain in the world!" Serious attempts did not begin until the early 1920's and it was only the accumulation of experience of successive expeditions to the mountain that finally culminated in the successful effort under John Hunt. The first path to the summit always seems the hardest, and now the Swiss have sent two two-man parties to the summit from Everest's South Col and another party to the top of tricky neighboring Lhotse, a truly great feat.

This is the way many mountains have been first climbed. Repeated failures have been the cairns by which paths to summits have been marked. It is the story of recorded mountaineering. From small hills to large, from foothills to high snows, from the Adirondacks to the Alps, from the Rockies to the Himalayas, climbers have pushed upward, been driven back, pushed again still higher until, at last, they have trodden the very crest of the world.

Recorded accounts of mountaineering start about 350 B. C. when it is said that Philip of Macedon climbed the Balkan Mount Haemus. He seems not to have received a royal reception, the summit being swathed in fog. A half millenium later, ascents of Mount Etna in Sicily became fairly common, Empedocles, a Greek philosopher, and the Emperor Hadrian numbering themselves among the adventurous. This climb to 10,739 feet probably set an altitude record for the age.

As trade and empire forged ahead routes across the passes of the Alps were found. Although not motivated by sporting instincts these mountain crossings often were creditable exploits, not the least spectacular being Hannibal's crossing with a herd of elephants. In the mid-fourteenth century the poet Petrarch climbed France's Mont Ventoux. While the ascent was motivated by the pleasure principle there is no evidence that he attempted other mountains. Even Leonardo da Vinci seems to have cast his eyes to the hills between experiments. Attempting Monte Rosa (15,217 ft.), Europe's second highest peak, he did not have the success that marked his other fields of endeavor.

It is sometimes forgotten that a quite remarkable ascent for its period was made in Mexico during the sixteenth century when some of Cortez' party climbed Mexico's Popocatapetl (17,852 ft.). The leader of the climb, Don Francisco Montano, was lowered four hundred feet into the active crater to collect sulphur for gunpowder! Today it is customary to attribute purer motives to climbers' efforts.

At the behest of France's Charles VIII precipitous Mont Aiguille, near Grenoble, was scaled with ladders in 1492. Even today there are fixed ropes there to assist climbers, hence it can be seen that the first ascent in the year Columbus discovered America is noteworthy. The idea of climbing mountains for fun received impetus from Conrad Gesner, a professor at the University of Zurich, who left a written account of his ascent of Pilatus, in 1555. Elsewhere he wrote that he meant "to climb Mountains, or at all events to climb one mountain every year."

In 1779, Canon L. J. Murith, of the Great St. Bernard Hospice, induced two chamois hunters to accompany him to the summit of Mont Velan (12,533 ft.). It was a notable enterprise, although that they reached the summit was due principally to the worthy canon's determination, his companions soon losing heart for the task.

By this time eyes had been lifted to Mont Blanc, the mighty massif southeast of Geneva which lies on the Franco-Italian border, its 15,772-foot summit crowning Europe. The name most intimately associated with Mont Blanc is that of Horace-Bénédict de Saussure, a Genevese naturalist, whose passion for the mountains dominated his life. It was his offer in 1760 of prize money for the first ascent of Mont Blanc that started a rash of attempts which resulted, over a quarter of a century later, in the successful climb of Dr. Michel-Gabriel Paccard and his porter, Jacques Balmat.

Although de Saussure garnered no significant "firsts," climbing for the most part where man had been before, his devotion to the mountains — a devotion that is said to have contributed to his death — was such that he is still regarded as one of mountaineering's greats. The year after the first ascent of Mont Blanc, he, too, made the climb. Today, in Chamonix, his statue stands looking up at the eternal snows.

At this period, and well on into the ninteenth century, it was fashionable to carry scientific instruments to the tops of mountains. The idea had not yet taken hold that normal people might climb mountains for pleasure. In the name of science, yes; but for sport? It is true that many interesting scientific observations were made, some of which have since proved useful, but lovers of the heights seldom confessed that science was not the only motivating force behind what was considered their folly.

It is common to refer to the mid-ninteenth century as the golden age of mountaineering. By then the Swiss had become aware of the mountains beneath which they lived. Summer after summer an increasing group of climbers, mostly British, but including Germans, French and Italians, was teaming up with Swiss guides to achieve a record of first ascents without parallel in mountaineering history. The fine tradition of guiding was getting its impetus from such men as Anderegg, Croz, Carrel, Bennen, Burgener, a tradition that still exists wherever mountains are climbed. The climax of the era came with the conquering of the Matterhorn (14,782 ft.), spectacularly and tragically highlighted by the disastrous descent that cost the lives of four of the seven-man party. The name of Edward Whymper will always be most closely associated with the Matterhorn for it was his belief, enthusiasm and persistence that culminated in the fateful climb of July 14, 1865. That day mountaineering came sadly of age.

Much remained to be done. During the latter part of the century Mummery set the pace, his brilliant climbing setting enviable records throughout the Alps. He was among the first to take mountaineering farther afield, going to the Caucasus, and later to the Himalayas where he disappeared in 1894 while assaulting Nanga Parbat. His imaginative daring can be seen in its true perspective by recalling that this fearsome mountain was not to succumb for another fifty years. Mummery was the first of the moderns and his name rests secure among the great.

As the 4,000-meter alpine peaks fell, men from all countries looked abroad. In Africa there were the Mountains of the Moon, in South America the forbidding peaks of the Andes. Climbers wondered about Alaska's Mount McKinley, rising 20,300 feet from the surrounding plateau, and they gave thought to the mighty Rockies of the United States and Canada. And there were always the incredible 8,000-meter giants of the Himalayan chain.

Aconcagua, the highest peak of the Andes, was first climbed by the Fitzgerald expedition of 1897. Not as difficult technically as some lesser peaks, its 23,080 feet presented no small problem. Ecuador's Chimborazo (20,697 ft.) had been ascended by Alexander von Humboldt as far back as 1802. Edward Whymper also did important work in South America, reporting on his explorations in his book *Travels Amongst the Great Andes of the Equator.*

Recently parties of young climbers from the United States have been making progress in South America. In 1950 Harrah and Maxwell, of the Harvard Andean Expedition, made the bitter ascent of Yerupaja (21,769 ft.), a mountain known more graphically as "the butcher." The boys did not escape unscathed. Harrah lost all his toes and Maxwell parts of three from frostbite. Two years later a similarly composed expedition went south again to tackle Peru's Salcantay (20,566 ft.) and the entire party reached the summit.

But what of mountaineering in North America? Where did it start and what have been its accomplishments? As civilization made its way westward across the United States and Canada, the pioneers had little occasion to think of climbing mountains for enjoyment. The problems facing them involved mountains; indeed, the tremendous rocky cordilleras presented imposing barriers to progress. Instead of going over the mountains, ways through them had to be found, a throwback to the days when the Alps had been breached via passes. If, as the American frontiersman pushed ever westward, he paused to climb a neighboring peak, it was the better to see what lay ahead, not to plant a barometer, not to jot down a description of the view, much less to claim a "first."

The intrepid Frémont, soldier, explorer and politician, violated this principle long enough to scale a 13,730 foot mountain in Wyoming's Wind River Range. In his honor, it has since been known as Frémont Peak. To the chagrin of Frémont, and his five-man party, neighboring Gannett Peak (13,785 ft.) proved to be the highest mountain in the area. Nevertheless, for 1842 the exploit was major mountaineering.

History records that one Chevalier de la Verendrye and his brother were the first white men to behold the Rocky Mountains, first espying the Bighorn Range on New Year's Day, 1738. During the eighteenth century most of the Pacific ranges were seen by navigator explorers.

They sailed the coastal waters as far north as Alaska, Vancouver discovering Denali, now known as Mount McKinley, while surveying Cook Inlet in 1794.

In 1811, geographer David Thompson pierced the Rockies via Athabasca Pass, thus opening a valuable route for the fur trade. It had been French fur traders who had named the magnificent Teton range in northwestern Wyoming. Attempts on the Grand Teton (13, 747 ft.) date back to 1843, but not until 1898 did Owen force a way to the summit by the route now named for him. Although there were conflicting claims as to the possible success of a climb in 1872, Owen's ascent has been authenticated as the first. The Grand Teton was not climbed again until 1923, and though the Owen Route is now considered the routine way to the summit, the first climb was a considerable effort.

All aspects of the Grand Teton have now been explored. It is now a popular playground, if hardly a safe place for inexperienced climbers. The East Ridge was accomplished by Henderson and Underhill and has been rated as equal to the stiffest climbs in Europe. In one of America's finest ascents, Fryxell and Underhill breached the great North Ridge in 1931.

Long's Peak (14,255 ft.) in the southern Rockies was one of the early gathering places for climbers. First ascended in 1868, hundreds went up the easy side during the next decade. The remarkable northeast face was first done in 1874 by Lamb. Although now quite popular, and offering varied possibilities, this face does not invite the beginner.

In northeastern United States' Cascade Range, Mount Rainier (14,408 ft.) stands supreme. An extinct volcano, covered with glaciers, it was climbed by Stevens and Van Trump in 1870. There is a curious rivalry between Rainier and California's Mount Whitney (14,495 ft.) in the Sierra Nevada. Because Whitney is the highest point in the country, it is the envy of admirers of Rainier. The suggestion has been made that if each climber of Rainier would carry up a large rock and deposit it on the summit, ultimately a large enough cairn would be raised to make Rainier higher than Whitney. An 87-foot cairn, of course, would be an imposing cairn.

Majestic Mount Robson (12,972 ft.) is the highest mountain in the Canadian Rockies, although not the highest mountain in Canada. Largely due to unpredictable weather Robson is treacherous and, during many summers, unclimbable. Mountaineers have been stalled only fifty feet from the summit by a gigantic overhanging cornice, surely a frustrating experience after a first rate ascent. The southern route on Robson is a high standard climb but any route will require the blessing of the elements. The first successful ascent was in 1913 by Foster and MacCarthy.

The mammoth St. Elias range stands athwart the international boundary. Mount Logan (19,850 ft.) and Mount St. Elias (18,024 ft.) have been the scenes of arduous mountaineering. Expeditions to this area have severe supply problems due to the long approaches required to even get on the mountain. Of the many attempts made on Mount St. Elias, the first to succeed was that of the Duke of the Abruzzi, Italian explorer and climber, in 1897. The expedition lived on glaciers and snowfields for a month and a half in order to force the successful ascent.

Mount Logan, east of the boundary in Yukon Territory, proved even tougher, resisting attempts on it until 1925. That year, an expedition of American, Canadian and British alpinists, under the determined leadership of MacCarthy of Robson renown, trod Logan's crest after an exceedingly difficult ascent. Nor were the difficulties over with the attainment of the summit. The withdrawal was painful in the extreme and it speaks much for the calibre of the party that it escaped the mountain without calamity.

Spectacular Mount McKinley, highest mountain on the North American continent, has been the scene of major expeditions, some of the more recent under Washburn being important scientifically. It is curious and humorous that the first near-successful climb on McKinley was made in 1910 by two prospectors. They may well have been the two most frustrated men in climbing history when they topped the North Peak only to perceive the South Peak some three hundred feet higher! Although their reckless exploit may now be tolerantly smiled on, it was an incredible effort, if hardly in the tradition of sound mountaineering. Two years later, Struck and Karstens climbed the South Peak. There have been a number of ascents in the intervening years, some by other routes, but a sufficient number of lives has been claimed by McKinley to warn that the climb of the two prospectors was a freak, that only a properly organized expedition belongs on those magnificent slopes.

Climbers of all nationalities have now joined the trek to the Himalayas, the abode of snow. Each year new honors are won: Annapurna by the French, Nanga Parbat by the Germans, K2 by the Italians, Lhotse by the Swiss, Kanchenjunga by the English. All efforts in the Himalayas are prey to the fickleness of the weather. Thus the successful Italian expedition to K2 in 1954 frankly admitted its debt to good weather for the summit dash. The ill-fated 1953 American attempt on that mountain suffered from heavy storms that marooned the party for ten days within striking distance of the top. Their retreat from the mountain was as difficult as the ascent and was marred by the tragic loss of Art Gilkey, one of the very fine crop of young American mountaineers. Thus do mountains sometimes exact a high price before yielding to men's onslaughts.

In 1950 Americans reconnoitered the southern approach to Mount Everest. This was significant to the mountaineering fraternity, the normal northern route being closed indefinitely by changes in the political climate of Tibet. The new route was the one used by the Swiss in their inspired but abortive effort of 1952, it was the way taken by the British in their victorious push the following year, and the path of the Swiss in 1956.

A bird's-eye view of an historical scene must perforce be disappointing to the person who craves facts and figures in detail. This summary does no more than touch lightly the tops of a few of the more prominent achievements. Mountaineering annals are filled with accounts of the exploits of men of all nations. Fully told, the tale is as glamorous, enthralling and stirring as an exciting piece of fiction but eminently more satisfying for its truth. He who has augmented his days on the crags with the reading of accounts of those who have gone before will be better equipped to make his own contribution to the constantly expanding volume of climbing lore.

Everest climbed? K2? Kanchenjunga? Lhotse? Yes, all climbed; but this is not the end of mountaineering. It is, rather, the beginning of a new era. The drama is in full development, great moments being recorded each year. Yet nothing is more precious to those climbers who make the history than, after their triumphs, to return with renewed affection to the well-known well-trodden ways.

Chapter 5

The Trail Is Up

*You must climb mountains on your
feet, and all your piety and wit
cannot cancel half a yard.*
BROOKS ATKINSON

EVERYBODY WALKS.

With the exception of those unfortunates who have in some way
been deprived of full use of their legs, the entire population walks. To
be sure, in this day of one automobile to every four people there is not
as much walking as there used to be. The corner mailbox, possibly a
mere two hundred yards distant, now seems to require use of the
family car rather than transit by the pedal extremities. Nevertheless,
every day everybody who arises from bed must do some walking.

The idea that the pleasure principle can be associated with walking
is retrogressing into the distant and nostalgic past. It is so much easier to
ride — walking takes so much time — and it's such an effort anyway.
Webster's Unabridged Dictionary implies that the sort of walking which
requires effort is really hiking. According to this perhaps it is no longer
true that everybody walks — it may more properly be said that everybody hikes.

It is important that anybody who feels impelled to climb a mountain quickly adjust to the fact that he is going to have to do it on his
own two feet, for whether it be labeled walking, hiking or climbing,
the act of continuously putting one foot before the other for an in-
definite period is the basic process by which summits are reached. At
this juncture it is probably necessary to part company with those who
cannot reconcile themselves to this premise. Some peaks, to be sure,
have been profaned by auto roads, mountain railways, teleferiques and
such; these will have to be the limit of exploration of that class of

"The trail is up."

"climber" who has so far succumbed to twentieth century mechaniza-
tion that the concept of eight to twenty hours afoot seems abhorrent.

Well, here's a trail. Let's take a walk.

Do you see that fellow up ahead? Going great guns, isn't he? A
regular hot shot. Don't be discouraged. Wait until this afternoon.
You'll see him again. He'll be sitting panting by the trailside while you
stroll by inquiring solicitously for his welfare. This chap, you see, com-
mits the cardinal sin of the trail: he feels fine early in the day, the
going is easy, his pack seems light, he fairly runs along. But he will
burn himself out before many miles have passed. He never heard of
the tenet of conservation of energy. He isn't going to have much reserve
for the homestretch. And you are.

You are, that is, if you are content to relax, to step along at what
seems almost too leisurely a pace, to adjust to the harshnesses underfoot
rather than to battle them, to find an easy rhythm and keep at it hour
after hour. The rhythm will be slower as you ascend, quicker as you
swing down the trail, but it will always be even, steady, unforced.

You will get the point later this afternoon when you see Mr. Hot
Shot begin to flag, his boots stumbling at rocks on the trail, his knees

stiffening. You will see him fall behind or hear him ask for repeated rests. But if you have maintained your rhythmically moderate stride all day you'll be feeling fit and may wonder what his trouble is.

The matter of uphill pace is crucial. It is astounding how many hours a mountain trail can go up, every step in defiance of gravity. The upward way won't stop until the summit, and while hands, arms and shoulders may be brought into use on the more difficult sections of rock, ice or snow, one foot is still going to have to move up in front of the other. Legs will feel indescribably heavy, muscles will rebel and cry for surcease, each step may become an act of will power, yet if the pace has been slow and steady, reserves will not be lacking, always provided that physical condition is good.

How to condition is another problem. Reserving for later discussion the problems of acclimatization and body conditioning, the question of how to make the legs fit for the task is vital. Intimately associated with the building up of leg endurance is the development of lung capacity. If the trail effort has been well-ordered there will not have been undue strain on the lungs. Breathing will have been rhythmical in direct proportion to the effort expended in climbing the trail. Thus the chap who raced ahead this morning will be panting as you pass him this afternoon whereas you will be breathing in more normal fashion and better able to adjust to and enjoy the keener air of the higher altitudes.

Simply, the way to condition for trail climbing is to get out on the trail and hike. If the region near you is studded with hills, so much the better. Select trails with plenty of ups and downs, extending your walks from week to week until you can comfortably manage twenty miles. Try to continue for long periods without resting, neither hurrying nor tarrying. Adjust your beathing to your pace and breathe deeply. This is how you will enlarge the capacity of your lungs. You will find that in the normal aspects of your living (unless you have a physically strenuous job) your breathing is surprisingly shallow.

You must develop lung capacity by conscious effort. Although the air of the city streets is not conducive to deep breathing, you can practice nonetheless, inhaling for six to eight paces, holding for two, exhaling for six to eight, and so on repeatedly as you walk in the course of your daily round. Not only will you thus improve your breathing for the mountain, you will be getting more oxygen into your blood where it is always needed for physical well-being.

There is a theory that running is the ideal training for climbing. Although the running track is flat a fast daily mile will benefit the leg muscles as well as help develop better respiratory facilities. Whether this will suffice when the trail is steep, rough and lengthy you will have to determine for yourself by trial and error. Tennis and swimming are useful training sports, too, but it is best not to be lured away from the open trail. The way to learn to play the piano is to spend hours at the keyboard.

Once you are on the mountain, walking will not necessarily be confined to a path. You will often deviate, either through choice or from necessity, from the well-marked trail. The nature of the going will alter markedly, requiring changes of pace. On sloping grass, for instance, the footing can be especially treacherous, particularly as the hillside steepens. Again, on any mountain of consequence it will be necessary to ascend scree or talus slopes. These are areas of loose rock that have broken away from the mountain. Not only must care be taken not to twist an ankle but you must be continuously on guard lest you roll a stone or stones back on your companions. In climbing such rocky slopes the party should break up so that one person does not climb directly behind another.

It might also be borne in mind that the descent of these loose stone slopes can be more dangerous than climbing up. While it is possible to glissade down loose scree, this is not recommended unless one is well practiced in the art. A fall, even if not disastrous, will tend to be mutilating.

It is important to make a distinction between walking on terrain that is more or less level and tackling steep trails on a mountainside. The principle of conservation of effort applies in either case, except that quite obviously more energy needs to be held in reserve for the long pull uphill. Therefore, the pace may seem unduly slow at first, particularly if the early going is level or of only moderate grade. It will soon become apparent, however, that this pace can be maintained with uninterrupted rhythm once the gradient becomes severe.

There must be no springing from toe to toe but rather a methodical placing of the whole boot on the ground. Ascending, the pace will become shorter but the basic rhythm will remain. Properly accomplished this kind of trail climbing can be kept up for hours on end. Surprising distances will be covered without there being any sense of exhaustion. As a trailside rest, a five-minute break every hour will be most welcome. When you reach higher and cooler altitudes, of course, you must be careful not to cool off too rapidly at such rest stops. Even when pausing only briefly it is wise to throw on a parka or sweatshirt.

Beginners assume that descending is easier than going up. There is usually a painful lesson in store to disabuse them of such thinking.

The experience often is a blithe ascent of a few thousand feet early in the climbing vacation, a pleasant reconnoitering climb as it were, then the start back down. But — wait a minute! What has happened? Those thigh muscles — they didn't feel like that coming up. And those knees — are they really moving in four directions at once? Every jolting step downwards becomes mildly excruciating. There must be something wrong.

Yes and no. What has happened, of course, is that the physical fitness with which you scampered up in the morning was just a burst of natural energy having nothing whatever to do with condition. Tomorrow the muscles used going up may be sore, too, but now many muscles not accustomed to the downward step and accompanying jolt are getting a working over. Not being used to such rough treatment, they are complaining loudly.

Actually, when the legs have been properly broken in, amazing things will happen on the downward trek. A trail that took five hours to ascend will be rapidly descended in an hour and a half. The pace will be a relaxed lope that uses gravity. A sharp eye must be kept when descending thusly so that the foot may be properly placed at each step. Tripping would be painful and perhaps dangerous. Once the art of going down the trail in this manner has been mastered, and the muscles have become properly adjusted to this kind of exercise, the descent to the valley may be accomplished with an exhilaration somewhat akin to that of skiing.

Any limbering exercises are helpful in getting the muscles prepared for the rigors of the trail. Try touching your toes a dozen or more times a day, gradually increasing the bend until you can touch the floor with your clenched fists. Do deep knee bends. In a deep knee bend position, with hands on hips and body erect, walk back and forth across the room. Try a few dance steps, Russian style, while in the same position. This will locate some forgotten muscles. Also recommended is stepping up and down on a chair, first with one foot, then with the other, even as in climbing. This can be practiced diligently until it is possible to have quite a climb without ever leaving your kitchen.

There are a few fundamental trail manners that may bear repeating. It is bad form to pass the leader or, indeed, to pass without reason anybody in your party who has taken a specific place in the line of march. If the one passed is somewhat slower than you he will doubtless take it unkindly, no matter how friendly or genial he may seem.

It should be equally obvious that it is unpleasant for the person in front if you persistently dog his heels. Since most steep trails permit only single file walking it is desirable to keep a fixed distance between you and the one in front. It is not your province to be concerned if the distance between such a climber and the party leader is lengthening. That is the leader's responsibility and he must be trusted to take cognizance of the situation.

Rope running through carabiners. When several are used, the rope will run more freely.

Should you be the first on the climb, the converse of the fore-going is especially applicable. Never outdistance those behind you. As leader on the trail you will set a pace that seems reasonable for your party, adjusting it if you are going either too fast or too slow. If, as is often likely, you are in better condition than the others, it is your duty to adjust to their condition, not to demonstrate your superior form. No one is more disruptive of harmony than he who fairly leaps up the trail, sits and awaits the others, then, just as they are almost abreast, leaps up and rushes on. He will be the recipient of "curses not loud but deep."

Wearying as the trek to the high hut or camp may be, this is only part of the job. Harder walking is still in store. There are ridges to be climbed, snowfields to be crossed, ridges and snowfields that mountain perspective may reduce to deceptive proportions. But distances in the mountains are measured in hours rather than miles. You will find that those ridges and snowfields sometimes seem to continue upwards ad infinitum. They will, if you are not adequately prepared, break your heart and spirit.

So in the spring, before you go to the high hills, get out on the open trail as often and for as long as you can. Give yourself repeated workouts, workouts that really tire you. Alternate running a hundred steps and walking a hundred. Load your knapsack heavily, adding some rocks if necessary. Do bushwhacking, eschewing the well-trampled trail. You will be glad later on that you did. There is an old saying that no matter how much or how hard you train for mountain climbing *nothing you do is ever enough.*

But how much better off you will be than the fellow who did nothing!

When the trail becomes so steep that hands and arms must be used you are leaving the realm of hiking and getting into stiffer climbing. But however exhilarating you may find the higher reaches of the mountain, do not look down upon, do not disdain, the trail up to the heights. Geoffrey Winthrop Young has said, "There is no doubt of the soundness of a man's climbing if he is seen to be a light and tireless hill walker."

If you would measure your mountaineering, here is your standard.

Chapter 6

The Accoutred Man

*The more a man possesses over and above what
he uses, the more careworn he becomes.*
GEORGE BERNARD SHAW

THE MOUNTAINEER'S clothing and equipment is for protection — protection against adverse weather and against the dangers of being in places where there is risk to life and limb. Comfort is most important, particularly as regards clothing, but safety is the cardinal principle. Clothing or equipment that does not contribute to physical or moral welfare is so much excess baggage, an encumbrance that may affect the success of the climb. It is desirable, therefore, to reduce the load to an essential minimum yet not to sacrifice anything that will be needed. The margin between these two means is narrow, definition often being a matter of personal taste. One mountaineer may want to travel light, ready to run a calculated risk of discomfort up high, while his partner may prefer to labor more on the lower trails so that he may enjoy extra comforts at the camp or hut. Although trial and error will determine for each what his minimum comforts need be, personal protection, whether against a penetrating wind on that north ridge or the precipitousness of an exposed pitch should be the factor that decides for or against a given piece of clothing or equipment.

There is no doubt that "going light" will permit more freedom and speed, and there are countless occasions when speed may well mean safety, but the price of going too light can be expensive, either in the mild terms of mere discomfort or the more serious perils of frostbite and worse. In paring down, therefore, plan carefully and beware of being caught short while high on your mountain. It could be much too costly an economy.

A climber reveres his boots. Sturdy boots that protect his feet from harm; dry boots, so constructed that water cannot penetrate; roomy boots, not so big as to be clumsy, yet large enough to allow for thick socks inside; comfortable boots that do not blister, bind nor chafe. Boots—the most important part of the mountaineer's equipment.

Left, rock climbing shoes; right, mountaineering boots with tricounis on heels.

For many years climbing boots had nails, hobnails, clinkers or tricounis, on sole and heel. Recently the nailed boot has almost disappeared in favor of cleated hard rubber. Sometimes a combination is used, such as tricounis for the heel and hard rubber for the sole, but whether they go by the name of Bramani, Vibram, Itshide, or whatsoever, hard rubber soles are here to stay, having revolutionized the mountaineering boot. A side asset to this conversion, which has largely taken place within the past decade, has been a welcome reduction of weight. Each pound less is that many foot-pounds less work en route to the peak.

Breaking in new boots can be a problem. Sometimes a new pair may be a natural, fitting easily and comfortably from the first moment, but the wails of climbers indicate that most new boots must become adjusted to the foot through a period that is more or less painful. Hours of use on the trail, however, seems to be the specific for ornery new boots.

An important feature is the hard-capped toe. This is primarily for protection from loose rocks that might fall on the foot doing injury that could jeopardize the well-being of a party, but it may also guard against the danger of a clumsily placed ice-ax. The boot's sole must not project beyond its outer contour, as on small footholds the weight of the foot should rest directly over the ledge. Any pair of boots made by a cobbler used to catering to mountaineers will not suffer from such fault.

A climber will cling fiercely to a good pair of boots, parting with them at last as with a beloved friend. He will treat them with reverence, using saddle soap liberally. He is aware that not only will a good pair of boots last longer (they are expensive enough at best), but he will be forestalling the day when it will become necessary to break in a new pair.

The best boots will be virtually without value unless good socks are worn. Various choices of socks will be worked out to taste, a sound combination for trail and mountain being a sturdy pair of medium weight next to the foot, with a heavy woolen pair worn over them. The foot will thus be kept both warm and comfortable. When boots are bought, the desired sock combination should be worn for the fitting so that boot size may be accurate. Extra socks must always be carried. If this practice is overlooked, the inability to replace damp clammy socks at day's end with dry fresh ones will probably be sufficient reminder for the future.

Various devices have been adapted to keep snow out of the boots, from army puttees to elastic gaiters. One of the most successful is the woolen gaiter that is wound, bandage style, spirally around the ankle and up the leg. On large expeditions trousers are sometimes specially designed so that the cuff may fit snugly over the boot top. It is not a problem that may be lightly dismissed, as snow in the boot is conducive to frostbite. There is small point to elaborately protecting the foot by good socks, only to ignore the influx of snow. The most desirable goal is to prevent moisture, whether water or snow, from entering the boots in the first place. It is more than likely, however, that climbers will continue to improvise with the usual indifferent success; but even if a 100 per cent resolution cannot be found, continued precaution will be well worth the effort and infinitely better than just surrendering to snow's infiltration.

There are those who wouldn't be caught loose in longies, woolen or otherwise, and pride alone is not the determining factor. Nearly any climber who decries wool underwear (be it red, white or whatsoever) will stoutly aver that it's a matter of allergy. Or just plain itch. Whatever alternative the red flannel dissenter may recommend, there's nothing to beat woolen undies when the north wind whistles. Going to great heights is akin to going to arctic or polar regions. This is true in the most vivid and accurate sense and should be the climber's basic clue as to how to accoutre himself for altitude.

Two requisites, somewhat contradictory in nature, must be taken into account. The undergarment shall be as heavy as necessary for maximum warmth, yet as lightweight as possible consistent with that warmth. Anything less than 50 per cent wool is inadequate. The drawback to a lightweight-maximum warmth garment will be its expense, yet the initial outlay may be compensated for many times over by its comfort.

A valid objection to "longies" is that they may be binding on the legs, restricting complete freedom of motion, particularly at the knees. They can be cut off just above the knees without sacrifice of comfort, although a well-made union suit will soon conform to the flexibility needed. It's also possible to buy just the top of a two-piece suit, making sure that it is long enough to come to the hips and cover the small of the back. Cotton shorts may then suffice, although here again individual taste as to comfort and requisite warmth will vary widely. But failing to prepare for proper body protection under the most severe circumstances may result in a spoiled climbing vacation, bodily injury, or even, as has happened to the uninformed or careless, death itself. It would hardly pay to let your first impromptu mountain bivouac be your last climbing experience.

So far we are standing in underwear, socks and boots. Humorous an image as this may conjure up, these are the basics, the minimums we cannot do without and over which price should be no object. However else the lily be gilded, and there are still essentials of prime order, lack of any of this basic three can be disastrous. There is no need to help the mountain make the problem more difficult.

For sake of the amenities, next in priority might be the climbing trousers. Here, custom plays an interesting part. Almost without exception, in England and on the continent, knickers, i.e., knee breeches, are the choice. These are generally of two varieties of cloth, either corduroy or closely-woven tweed. Durability is important, particularly at seat and knees, and sometimes there is lining at the knee as well as at the seat. The latter feature is of particular comfort when sitting on snow, ice or cold rock. As corduroy has a tendency to retain moisture and become unduly heavy, it is perhaps the second preference, although continental guides favor it. Taste may determine choice but as between tweed and corduroy either will do if well-made and durable. Pennies saved in poorer texture will be dollars lost in early purchase of another pair of knickers.

American mountaineers have a penchant for long trousers with an elastic cuff at the ankle. This can be a virtue in snow, although the leg of the garment should be full-cut despite the tapering at the ankle. Anything with restrictive action must be avoided. As in all clothing for the mountains, protection of the most durable yet flexible kind is to be adopted. With the knicker, of course, knee-length socks are necessary, elasticized at the top. A slipping stocking is as distracting to a mountaineer as to a well-dressed woman.

Walking shorts are often worn, particularly on the lower mountain when temperature and climate permit. Some simply don trousers over the shorts when colder altitudes are reached or in inclement weather. This useful device has the additional virtue of further comfort and protection when sitting. One pair of trousers and a pair of hiking shorts will be sufficient for the average climbing holiday. On an expedition the problem is more complicated, and the judiciousness of extra clothing must be appraised accordingly. Weight, under either circumstance, is a potent consideration.

Protection of the upper body from cold is a peculiarly vexing problem. There is a well-tried theory that several layers of light clothing are better than one heavier garment. The idea is that the air between layers becomes warm and acts as an insulating barrier. There is no reason to doubt this principle; but since concepts vary, alternatives may be considered.

A light, closely woven garment is probably preferable to a heavier, loose one. Predicating heavy underwear as being next to the skin, one or two shirts, according to temperature, with, perhaps, a pullover sweater, can be quite protective. Sometimes various layers of light sweaters, or polo shirts, are used to absorb excessive perspiration. This question of sweating is a major consideration for it is necessary to keep as warm when resting or standing still during the climb as when active. *Sudden cooling off must be avoided.*

The wind wreaks most havoc with the climber's comfort; hence, however skillfully the body has been protected by underwear, sweaters, shirts and pullovers, a windbreaker must be available. A zippered nylon jacket, with hood for the head, has the advantage of lightness although the heavier poplin parka may be sturdier. Whichever the choice, there should be good closure at the throat, a deficiency of too many parkas. Only a scarf can compensate for this lack. Zippered pockets are helpful and drawstrings will make it possible to close the hood snugly as well as to take in the waist.

Down jackets are coming into their own. Although they look impossibly bulky they can be rolled into very small compass, they are light as the feathers they are made of and extremely warm. The outer fabric, usually gaily colored nylon and elastic at the waist and wrists, makes for snugness. Being expensive, the down jacket may be looked upon as a luxury but the warmth it affords in the bitterest cold is its own reward and at high camp it can be as comfortable as the comforter it so closely resembles.

At all costs, the body must be kept warm. It is better to wear too much than too little, even at the expense of a heavier knapsack. Judicious selection of clothing, however, according to your experienced needs, can mitigate against unnecessary overloading. The chief thing is to keep warm at rest stops, to cool off slowly, to sustain circulation. The extremities, fingers and toes, are soonest subject to frostbite. If, having been cold to the danger point, the fingers or toes begin to be unnoticeable, it may be that frostbite is setting in. Immediate attention will be necessary, whatever the circumstances. If in a forced bivouac, putting the feet in a knapsack, boots and all, may make much difference. There's also a theory, particularly dear to the British, that newspaper wrapped around the midsection next to the skin can be most helpful when prolonged inaction at high, cold altitudes is a prospect. It has never been made quite clear, however, where the newspaper conveniently comes from.

Headgear of some sort is always necessary at high altitudes. Mountaineers being individualists, the assortment of caps, hats or what-have-yous found on any self-respecting mountain will be various. In choosing for style, however, it is wise to recall that the hat, like other gear, is for protection. A hat with a brim in front (hence cap or ski-cap) will be useful for protecting the eyes and face from the sun although the peak should not be too large, particularly where rock-work is to be done. Since protection of the ears is needed, particularly in a cold wind, a hat with flaps to pull down is useful. For arduous conditions appearance is nothing, protection all, and this should be a sober consideration when getting that headgear.

Gloves are a must. In rock climbing there isn't much for it but cold hands, although gloves with fingers cut out may afford trifling protection. Since it's the fingers that suffer most, however, the compromise is dubious. Woolen mittens will be useful at high altitudes where the cold may be intense. If they get wet it is a difficult choice between the cold of wet frozen mittens or no gloves at all. Sometimes a waterproof pair of mittens may be drawn on over the woolen.

On snowfields and glaciers dark goggles will be worn. Without them, snowblindness would result. They should fit closely to the bone structure, being covered where contacting the face. To prevent steaming, there should be air vents around the side. Ordinary summer sunglasses will not do, as too much reflection can get in at the sides and bottom. Proper goggles are inexpensive at any mountaineering equipment store.

A rucksack is a prerequisite. If it can be simultaneously sturdy and lightweight, this will be a boon. There are as many kinds of rucksacks as there are manufacturers of them, but the summit sack should be large enough to hold the necessary extra clothing, whatever food is required, emergency first aid equipment, as well as photographic gear if pictures are planned.

For the higher mountain a frame rucksack is not desirable. Although excellent for toting from valley to high camp, the summit sack cannot be as unwieldy. It may have to be hauled up or let down rock pitches, it must fit the body snugly and closely. It needs to be durable, and while nylon is satisfactory weight-wise, duck will wear better. Either should be waterproof. At least two pockets should be on the outside of the pack. If the straps or zippers can be handled without taking off the mittens, this is a plus. A too small pack is bad as it will always be too crowded. A larger sack partially filled will be more practical and the weight will be better distributed.

The mountaineer who always carries an overloaded rucksack can brag that at one time or another everything has come in handy, often for somebody else. This is often the case, and a slight overage is better than not having the extra piton or additional socks or goggles when emergency befalls, but just as selectivity is the soul of art, so a judicious weeding out before the big climb is a sage precaution. Determine which are your prime essentials and which the secondary for your maximum comfort and minimum load. Among the irreducibles, excluding food, would certainly be: extra socks; sweater; shirt or shirts; extra gloves; spare boot laces; knife; sunburn lotion; compass; puttees or gaiters; wool scarf; handkerchiefs; maps; notebook and pencil; matches; towel; flashlight; first aid basics such as moleskin for blisters, adhesive tape, aspirin, gauze, elastic bandage. Secondaries will be luxuries and must be included or rejected according to your willingness to encumber yourself with extra weight. One extra pound will be an extra 10,000 foot pounds of work between Zermatt and the summit of the Matterhorn.

To the mountaineer it seems incredible that people still think the climbing rope is to haul one up a mountain. Knowledge of climbing technics has spread so in recent years that the informed looks askance at the kind of humor exemplified by, "How does the first guy get up there — Indian rope trick?" The weary climber is likely to respond that it's all done with anti-gravitational pills.

120-foot nylon rope, ½-inch diameter. Angle piton. Oval carabiner (aluminum). Sling rope (or waist rope for carrying "hardware").

Let the record be set straight: the function of the rope is to protect the climber; it is for safety. It is the bond that binds the climbing party together, no party being stronger than the weakest climber on the rope. Sometimes it may be necessary to give a tight rope to a weak or tiring member of the climbing team, but the rope's primary function is to protect, to safeguard. In the type of climbing sometimes labeled steeplejacking, in which the ascent is made by a complicated system of pitons

Coiling the rope.

and carabiners, with almost constant tension on the rope to sustain the leader, the rope is definitely a direct aid, but this type of climbing is for the specialist and in no way modifies the rope's essential function.

Length and diameter of the rope varies from country to country and even between tastes of individuals. Generally, however, $\frac{7}{16}$-inch is satisfactory, and 120 feet is a good length. Exceptions are one-half inch rope for rock climbing where the rope will be subjected to rugged use for club purposes, or with novices who may put more than average

strain upon the rope. In Europe a rope slightly less than ⁷⁄₁₆-inch diameter is used, something comparable to our own ⅜-inch, but which most Americans think too thin. The length can vary, and where a long rappel (roping down) is a prospect a 150-foot rope will be an advantage. For a two-man party, an 80-foot rope occasionally may be used.

Nylon is the rope of choice. Hemp was the traditional climbing rope but, with the advent of nylon which boasts elasticity vs. brittleness, long life vs. short, flexibility vs. stiffness, nylon has carried the day. One of its greatnesses is its ability to stretch at the point when hemp would break. Tests on nylon have shown that it can be stretched to almost filament thinness, although the impact of a fall would be decisive long ere that. The danger of a fall is no longer of the rope breaking but of damage to the climber. A heavy fall may result in cracked or broken ribs from the rope or serious internal injury (discounting for the moment the dangers of striking objects during the fall).

The climbing rope has the faculty of communication. By this is not meant the series of tugs that is sometimes devised to telegraph intent when climbers are out of sight of each other, but rather the intangible something that relays itself up and down the rope between climbers and by which they often instinctively know whether all is good or ill. To a well-adjusted climbing team, the rope will be not only a physical bond for the safety of all, but a psychological factor that will ensure better communication, better climbing and better esprit. It is wise to learn to use the rope with affection, care and sensitivity from the outset of a climbing career because its claim is valid as a climber's best friend.

The ice-ax is second only to the rope as a climbing auxiliary. Its use is severalfold: step-cutting, belaying, probing, glissading, occasional direct aid, balance as a "third" leg or arm. Specifics of ice-ax use will be dealt with later, but some knowledge of what to look for when purchasing is in order.

Firstly, it should be of straight-grained ash or hickory. Slightly shorter than a walking cane is the correct length, allowance being made for the ferrule's sinking slightly into the ground or snow. The point of the ax should be 6″ to 7″ long, the adze about half that length. A running ring with a wrist sling may be helpful, although opinions vary sharply as to its usefulness and desirability. A good piece of leather looped over the head and around the shaft is probably as effective.

The ax should balance about 9″ from the head. When it must be used for a firm belay in deep snow or on ice, it is imperative that it be strong throughout its length. As with rope and boots, compromise with quality is not advisable. The notches on the underside of the blade serve no practical purpose and may be disregarded. In storing the ax between climbing seasons, it is well to use linseed oil on the wood and vaseline on the metal. The weight of a satisfactory ax should not exceed three pounds.

For climbing on ice or hard-crusted snow, crampons are required. Not only do they make possible the ascent of ice slopes not otherwise accessible, they vastly reduce the time of a climb by saving the cutting of innumerable steps. The ten-point crampon is typical, although eight-point crampons are used (as are crampons with from four to nineteen points.) A light crampon is also now available, although it has not the durability of the older and heavier model. It has the inestimable virtue, however, of saving many foot-pounds of work on the climb. Any mountaineer who has cramponned upwards for long hours will vouch for the desirability of lightness.

Rope, ice-ax, crampons and sun goggles.

Crampons must be carefully adjusted to fit the boot, being patterned to the boot's outline, the points going down directly at the boot's edge. When the straps are tightened the crampon should seem an integral part of the shoe.

"Hardware" is the colloquial name for pitons and carabiners (or snaplinks) which are the basic equipment for protecting climbers on stiff rock or ice. Pitons are simply flat pieces of tapered steel with eyes in the end. These can be driven into cracks in rock, or driven and frozen into ice and snow. When they have been wedged or driven in firmly enough, carabiners can be snapped into the eye and the rope passed through the snaplink.

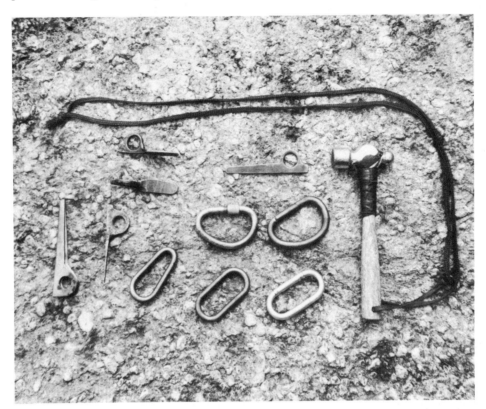

Rock climbing "hardware." Hammer and shoulder sling. Vertical, horizontal and angle pitons. Oval, pear- and D-shaped carabiners, both aluminum and steel.

Carabiners are made of either steel or aluminum. The gate should have a spring sufficiently strong to keep the carabiner closed on the piton and to keep the rope securely enclosed and able to run freely. Aluminum carabiners are as strong as steel and for lightness of carry are preferable. As aluminum is usually thicker, however, it is prudent to have a couple of steel snaplinks handy for those pitons in which the eye has been driven in so far that insertion is difficult. Where a piton's protection is needed is no place to have to search for the proper carabiner.

A hammer is necessary for pounding pitons into place. An ordinary ball peen hammer is good, though it may be advisable to have a hammer with a point at one end for ice work. The pointed hammer, however, is destructive of clothing, particularly of the pocket in which it may be carried. A long loop of leather thong must go from the hammer handle over the shoulder so that the hammer may not be lost in use. Its loss could seriously handicap the climb as well as jeopardize the safety of climbers below.

Handling a carabiner.

In summary, when buying clothing and equipment, *do not compromise with quality*. A few dollars spent at the outset may save in comfort and safety and possibly make the difference between a satisfactory or unsatisfactory climbing holiday. Let the best be good enough for you.

Chapter 7

On The Rocks

Prove all things; hold fast to
that which is good.
ST. PAUL

IF MOUNTAINEERING breeds a degree of rugged individualism, then that part of the sport in which man pits himself against the realities of stubborn rock is probably climbing at its mettlesome best. True, there is easy rock and there is difficult rock, but there is also varying form, today's easy scramble becoming tomorrow's exhilarating struggle. Again, weather can convert a moderate pitch into a touchy climb, for nothing is more treacherous than wet rock and nothing more forbidding than cold. Let a good mountaineer, off his form, be confronted with chilly slippery rock and he will doubtless retreat while in good order, for he knows that another day this same pitch will seem straightforward. The careless novice, on the other hand, might feel impelled by false courage to move forward anyway. It is just this ability to distinguish between the courage of retreat and the foolhardiness of advance that may mark the success or failure of a mountaineering career. The technics of climbing can be explained, demonstrated, practiced and thus acquired. Good judgment cannot.

These generalizations are equally pertinent to climbing on ice and snow, but faith in one's ability to solve a sticky rock problem seems to be the greater trap for the unwary. It is easy to admonish "Never move forward unless sure you can get back" but there's scarcely a rock climber who wouldn't, if pressed, admit that he had sometime suffered personal embarrassment from failing to follow this commonly simple stricture. The morose corollary is that there have been less fortunate brethren who have also forgotten or ignored this elementary tenet, bringing disaster upon themselves and an unworthy reputation to the sport.

There are philosophies about the use of pitons and carabiners that should be briefly examined. Varying approaches to the sport are manifested by various nationalities. The English, as a case in point, are purists, considering "hardware," or any form of artificial aid in climbing, to be abominations. It is said that in all the magnificent rock climbing territory in North Wales, for example, only a single piton adorns the cliffs. Contrariwise, German climbers revel in overcoming all obstacles. To this end they scale the unscalable, using pitons, rope tension, rope slings, and even aluminum rungs that can be pounded in small cracks to make possible the ascent of otherwise insurmountable walls.

Placing a rock piton.

Although Americans indulge in a certain amount of such steeple-jacking, their overwhelming preference is to use piton and carabiner arrangements *for safety only,* not for direct aid, on the theory, perhaps, that mountaineering is more fun if spread over the span of a normal lifetime. This approach is a middle road, a cross between asceticism and gymnastics, yet rock problems being solved in the United States today are parallel to those anywhere in the world.

It is necessary to rope up, that is to tie into the climbing rope, as soon as the rock angle requires constant use of the hands. Thus, scrambling up talus slopes needn't call for tying in, but when the ascent becomes anything more than an easy scramble the rope must be used for safety. Only when the degree of severity is inordinately difficult, when the climber has exceeded his ability, or when there is a fall, however, should the rope be used for an assist.

The knot of choice is the bowline and will be used by climbers at each end of the rope. It should be well-practiced for it must be second nature to tie oneself in under any conditions. Scouters may remember how to tie the bowline from the doggerel, "the rabbit comes out of the hole, goes around the tree and back in the hole," the hole being a loop in the rope, and the tree the piece of rope that extends away from the body. The waist rope should be very snug (some say as tight as a girdle) and enough slack should be allowed at the end so that several half-hitches can be taken around the waist loop after the knot has been tied. When the rope is worn for a long time, the knot should be checked periodically lest it become loose.

The middleman's knot can be either a simple overhand loop or the more complicated butterfly. Although the overhand knot is used most commonly, the butterfly is preferable because the rope leads into and away from the knot in such fashion that there is little danger of cutting or breakage at the point of tie in event of a fall.

For joining two ropes together the fisherman's knot (or bend) should be learned. It is extremely simple and should occasion no difficulty, although an extra half hitch is important at each side as insurance. The square knot should be known, but it is not useful when tied in slippery nylon. This "slipperiness" of nylon must constantly be considered, as knots may work loose.

If the party is wearing the rope on simple rock and moving simultaneously, several coils of rope may be carried in one hand so that a little may be taken in or let out if the pace of each climber should vary. This is also standard practice on glaciers and snowfields. When the rock is steep enough for only one climber to move at a time, however, the rope will be paid out or taken in carefully.

Under whatever circumstances, the rope must always be used with circumspection. It is a lifeline, and nicks, cuts, breaks or badly frayed spots will diminish its value if not make it virtually worthless. You should never stand on the rope or permit heavy objects to fall on it. You should handle the rope and protect its life with something approaching reverence. Since a good climbing rope is expensive, this

How to tie a bowline around the waist and how to secure it.

is another graphic reason for care, if not the primary one. Nylon is rugged, wears well, has elasticity, but its superiority to hemp is not an invitation to abuse.

There are three kinds of footgear common to rock climbing. As part of getting up the mountain, the climbing boot is indicated, of course. For fine rock work, however, it may prove clumsy, and where rock climbing is a specialty, as in Italy's Dolomites, Chamonix, France,

or parts of the United States, either rubber-soled sneakers or a thin-soled lug climbing shoe are worn. The latter has become increasingly popular and has the advantage of being almost as effective on wet rock as on dry. While these shoes are more expensive than sneakers, they have the virtue of longer life and make it possible to stand on tiny nubbins of rock that would refuse the sneaker. Sometimes in high mountaineering it is wise to pack a rock climbing shoe in the rucksack if it is known that particularly thin pitches will be encountered.

For wet rock, the rope-soled shoe had long and distinguished use, but the advent of lug-soles has made the scarpetti archaic. In getting a rock climbing shoe or sneaker, a tight fit is required so that the foot may be placed on diminutive holds with assurance. Not quite the same confidence can be placed in the sturdier mountaineering boot because the foot's "feel" of the rock is lost.

A mark of the rock-climbing novice is overuse of the arms and shoulders. Progress then takes on the aspect of a wrestling match, a

titanic struggle between mismatched forces. Contrast such climbing with the smooth, almost catlike ascent of a skilled climber and it seems incredible that the same problem is involved. What is the secret of the expert's seeming lightness and the beginner's obvious heaviness? Is there hope for the eager beaver debutant?

As in all phases of activity, some people have a flair and some do not. A taste for the sport is not synonymous with ability to pursue it. Nevertheless, many an incompetent duffer has been trained into a

cragsman of better than moderate skill, and there must be a reason why this has been accomplished.

The novice's first mistake is to rely too much on arms and shoulders, neglecting the support his normally stronger legs can give him. The weighty work should be done by the legs, the arms and hands being used primarily for balance. There will be times, as in surmounting an overhang, when maximum strength is demanded of arms and shoulders, but unless the legs have been bearing the burden until that

point is reached, there may not be strength enough left for the "chinning" task. The hands and arm muscles must be relied on for many purposes but not for dragging a climber up a cliff. This lesson must be learned early and forever; it will save many a weary struggle.

Balance is all-important. It is essential to keep the body weight as directly over the feet as possible; in other words, the climber should remain as nearly erect as the pitch and difficulty of the rock will permit. Timidity's tendency is to flatten in to the cliff, to embrace it if possible. This is unwise and unsafe. The closer the body gets to the rock the more the feet will tend to slide off the footholds. Difficult as it may seem at first, the rule is to stand up, to be able to look around, to place the feet for support, the hands for balance. There should always be space between the body and the cliff. It may sometimes be necessary to literally crawl around a projection or along a shelf, but these are exceptions.

A further advantage of the erect position is that such stance enables the climber to use his eyes to search for holds and route. It is a wise climber who remembers the holds long enough so that the feet may automatically choose those which have been recorded mentally when at eye level. Most often, when the body has worked up a few

Making use of a small foothold.

feet, perfectly good stances for toe or foot are no longer easily visible. Memory of holds the eye has seen and the hands used will reduce time and effort lost while the foot scrabbles about for the elusive niche or nubbin. Such foresighted selectivity is invaluable as an economy measure, for every bit of energy conserved through considered climbing is that much in store for whatever may lie ahead.

A basic rule is to always keep three points of contact with the rock, either two hands and a foot or two feet and a hand. Anything less is risky, particularly if in motion. Many a mistake has been made when a hand and a foot have been moving at the same time. Should a slip occur, or should a relied on piece of rock give way, there is practically no protection, and a futile grab is less than nothing. Anybody who has had the experience of rock giving way, even when he is firmly anchored, knows the sickening feeling and will readily understand this rule. It is wiser, of course, to accept the axiom than to test it. Needless to add, lunging or jumping for a hold is extremely dangerous and in the poorest form. The question need only be put, "What if you miss? . . ."

Much has been made of rhythmic climbing. There is no doubt that a well-coordinated climber moving steadily up a cliff is pleasant

Balance on a slab.

to behold; there is a clear rhythm to his movements. Probably, however, the smoothness and rhythm come after the fact. The proper way
to master the art is to move slowly when learning, letting each step
and hold be part of a developing pattern, practiced deliberately and
carefully until, by imperceptible degrees, the pace may be stepped up.
Not that fast rock climbing is ever desirable; it is rather a case of
making haste slowly. The skilled climber, moving easily, is progressing

"Balance is all important."

apace because he has mastered the art of almost constant, yet controlled, motion. Even his pauses seem part of the pattern, and when, after due consideration, he makes a difficult move, it is certain that he will do it with grace and safety. Rushing the rocks just won't do and many a Mr. Hot Rocks has foundered early because he has not been content to realize that the long way round is often the shortest way home.

While it has been indicated that the principal use of the hands is for balance, this is somewhat of an over-simplification. The harder the climb, the more the hands will be used for staying on the climb, although the hands shouldn't cling to the rock as much as give the necessary assist, whether of pull, push, jam or balance.

Apart from balance, the pull will be the prime use and it is important to see that the pull is downward on the ledge and not outward. Except in certain technics such as the layback or underhold, pull on the rock should not be away from the cliff lest the hand slip off the hold or the rock break. An advantage of the pull-down is that it can often be converted into a push-up as the body rises. This makes it possible to move the other hand higher to another hold, at which time the first hand may again be moved up. The transition must be made carefully, but if done with finesse when the ledge is large enough for the heel of the hand the motion can be an easy flow. It is wrong, however, to get both hands into the push-up position simultaneously as such position is not well-balanced and is particularly difficult to get out of if the rock is steep.

When the hands can push against opposite walls of rock, or when they can squeeze on opposite sides of a projection, the push principle comes into play in a different direction than downward, with both hands in opposition providing the sustaining force. The reverse of this obtains when each hand pulls away from the other as in climbing a narrow crack. In a crack, the hand may be jammed, or a fist may be made and jammed. As each of these technics is called upon, it is well to understand the principle and to practice as often as possible, not being satisfied with just "getting up" but going back down over awkward steps and repeating for smoothness. On slabs, the mere pressure of the palm of the hand on the smooth rock may provide the retaining power, friction being what holds the hand in place. In such climbing, the palm is down, the fingers pointing to the side or down, rarely upward.

Placement of the feet is determined by the nature of the problem. On a sizeable ledge the feet are in the normal standing position, adjusting, if necessary, to any slope of the rock. If the ledge is small, so that just the toe or side of the foot can be used, care must be taken that the placement be exact and without slippage. It is on the small ledge or toehold that the importance of having boots without projection becomes manifest.

Walking across a slab. Feet are flat, body's center of gravity remains vertical.

In crack climbing it may be possible to jam the toe of the boot into the crack, either directly or sideways, depending upon the crack's width. This is where the sneaker or rock climbing shoe is superior to the mountaineering boot. Care must be taken not to jam the shoe in so hard that it is difficult to extricate, for by the time the body has moved up from its original position too much strain will come on the hands, too much effort will be expended in trying to free the foot and balance may be jeopardized.

The principle on slabs is the same for feet as for the hands, friction alone supporting the body. It is particularly important on slabs that the centre of gravity be kept as fully as possible over the feet. Any attempt to cling to the rock will result in slippage. When learning, it is often hard to convince oneself of this, but practice on slabs of varying inclination, preferably near the ground, will teach the needed lesson.

The body itself is seldom used as a climbing adjunct. Its function is primarily for balance, the weight being distributed in as direct a line as possible over the feet. In climbing overhangs, it may be necessary and comforting to use the friction of the body against the rock. In slab-climbing, if a slip occurs, the friction of the body against the rock may help arrest a fall provided the slab isn't too steep, but this is not a recommended safeguard.

Great discretion is required when placing pitons. Since a piton's prime purpose is protection of the leader, a piton should be used whenever wisdom deems it necessary, yet the cliffs should not be festooned with iron-mongery. There are three basic types of rock pitons, the horizontal, vertical and angular. Generally the last is the soundest, but it requires a larger crack. All three types come in various lengths, and the horizontal piton also varies in width, some being almost like a spoon.

Whichever type is used, as dictated by the size of and shape of the crack, it should be pounded in well. A well-placed piton is always recognizable by the high ring it gives when struck. When a leader, for example, comes to a piton placed in the cliff by a preceding party, he can test its safety for use by hitting the head with his hammer. If the pitch is high, the piton may be adjudged safe. Sometimes, however, pitons are tested by hitting them sideways or up or down. This is inadvisable, as it may only loosen or weaken an otherwise safely placed protection.

Questionably placed, or questionably sounding, pitons should never be relied on. If it is possible to remove the doubtful offender, by all means do so. If not, it ought to be hammered all the way into the crack to prevent further use, or otherwise mutilated. Oddly, some pitons that cannot be hammered out may be wiggled back and forth gently with the fingers and thus slowly removed. But *never* trust a piton you are not sure of.

There is an infinite variety of rock climbing problems and they are as various as the nature of rock itself. Certain basics are common to most climbs, and they occur either alone or in combination. Some of the problems that will be encountered are those described below

Chimneying.

and the ability to recognize and cope with each as met is a mark of the successful cragsman.

GULLIES. Gullies were the route of choice when men first started climbing rock. They are generally easier problems than other aspects of rock climbing, the rock tending to be more broken up so that more holds are available. This advantage is offset in wet weather when the gully is a watercourse, and the water may have made the rock smoother. Gullies are frequently damp, anyway, being recessed from the sun. There is less height exposure, however, an advantage for the novice. Rock in gullies may be loose, so not only must the climber be alert to the danger of falling stones, he must beware of knocking them down on others, gullies being the natural chute for rocks or snow. *In the climbing lexicon, there is no excuse for dislodging rock.*

The technic varies, of course, with the problem within the gully. Since there may be satisfactory holds, it is mostly a question of working slowly upward. Slabby pitches may be encountered, and these may be solved by direct attack. If this is not possible, it may be feasible to work up one side or other of the gully until the tricky bit has been by-passed. There is no formula for gully-climbing, however, as the technics demanded will tend to be any or all of those which follow.

CHIMNEYS. In a sense, chimneys are narrow, mostly vertical, gullies. Indeed, gullies often contain chimneys, or the gully itself may even narrow to chimney width. The technic depends on the chimney's

Straddling a chimney.

width and on the nature of the rock, whether it be rough or smooth.
If wide, the chimney may be straddled, the right hand and foot pushing

Climbing a crack. Notice use of feet. Shortly he will lay back to the left.

against one wall, the left hand and foot against the other. There are sometimes small holds within the chimney and these can be advantageously used. A somewhat narrower chimney can be forced by placing the back against one wall, the feet against the other; by pushing with hands, back and feet by turns, it is then possible to edge upward steadily. A variation of this technic is placing one foot backward beneath the buttocks, the other foot on the opposite wall, placing the hands in similar, but higher, opposition. Which method is most convenient will depend on width of chimney, size of climber and even the climber's taste.

If the chimney is too narrow to bridge as above, it will be necessary to use the body to a greater extent. Sometimes the chimney will only be wide enough for the climber to stand upright in. This is cramped climbing and the hands and feet must be used as convenient or as possible. Body friction may help, although it may also make the ascent more difficult.

With the possible exception of overhangs, chimneys require more physical exertion than most rock work. Constant pressure on opposite sides of the chimney *must* be maintained. A slip in a chimney is nearly impossible to arrest. It is necessary, therefore, to move carefully and cautiously, to think before each move, to rest where safety will allow. Too long a rest in chimney position, however, can be tiring, and it is wise, if possible, to keep moving to the top.

CRACKS. Gullies can narrow to chimneys and chimneys to cracks. Cracks in rocks can also exist independently and it is surprising how often a seemingly impossible rock face will be rent by a vertical crack that becomes the key to its ascent.

In the average crack, hands and toes of the boot are all that can be used. For this reason, cracks are usually a grade or two more difficult than other problems. The body has to be balanced delicately, keeping the center of gravity as directly as possible over the feet. If the crack is narrow enough, the hand-jamming toe-jamming technic is probably the best. The hands, however, may grasp opposite sides of the crack, pulling in opposition, or, if there are rugosities available at either side of the crack (and such holds, even though small, should be watched for) these may be used advantageously. Any rugosities at either side of the crack which are useful for the hands may be equally so for the feet when they reach that level. Sometimes it is possible to lay back sideways to the crack, with the hands pulling against one side, the feet pushing against the other, in opposition to the hands. It is not always easy, however, to regain a vertical position after such a manoeuvre. Since cracks are as hard, if not harder, to climb down, be sure that a line of retreat is available.

CORNERS. Verschneidung is the German name for the inside corner of a cliff. There are difficult verschneidungs and easy verschneidungs, but the technic of ascent is similar. It is usually possible to use simultaneously both faces of the rock forming the corner. While it may be necessary to use one face or other at some phase of the climb, the easiest route is generally in the corner itself. Again the layback may be handy, but it will not often be the method of ascent of the entire pitch. The assortment of holds may vary but a corner is frequently a very nice climb because something to use can generally be found and there is a good sense of upward progress. Modified chimney technics will also be found applicable in the verschneidung.

LAYBACKS. Laybacks have already been described as possible solutions to crack and corner problems. Sometimes a stretch of rock is encountered wherein the layback is the only solution. The hands are placed behind the corner of the rock, the feet are placed against the rock face within reasonable proximity of the hands, depending on the climber's height. Then, by alternately moving a hand, a foot, and so continuing, the layback pitch is mounted. The strain on the hands and arms is tiring, so it is wise to see the pitch through in one stretch if possible. Too fast can be as tardy as too slow, in which event there is a tendency for the hands to "outwalk" the feet, precipitating a fall from the layback position. Until the layback technic has been thoroughly mastered it is wise to consciously dictate the individual moves of each hand and each foot. Three points of contact are, of course, paramount.

FACES. There is no more exhilarating feeling in climbing than that of working up a thin rock face. It may not be too much to say that it is the next thing to walking on air.

All faces are not thin and it is wise to become familiar with face climbing technic where holds are plentiful and spacious. The use of the body is most important. This may sound odd as the body is never in contact with the rock. It is the balance, however, the shifting of weight that is significant. Sometimes it is even necessary to climb sideways to the cliff, particularly if the route goes off to right or left. On steep rock, crossing from one thin foothold to another off to the side can be considerably more delicate than moving straight upward. The boot must be placed precisely and surely and each handhold must be chosen and used with care. "Handhold" is a misnomer for much face climbing, fingerhold being the more apt term. The nervous fingers examining the rock with almost a caress are familiar to every rock climber.

It is worth reiterating that it is important not to climb beyond the point of no return. Where the balance is a matter of such delicacy it will be infinitely harder to descend. The route of ascent, therefore, the pace and method shall be worked out with utmost precision if the pitch is difficult. It is in thin face work that the superior cragsman truly comes

A layback.

into his own, and to watch him work his way up with catlike stealth can be exhilarating even in the beholding.

OVERHANGS. To the casual observer, the most impressive rock climbing feat seems to be the surmounting of overhangs. Actually, overhangs range from simple to impossible. If the holds above the overhang are good, and if the rock doesn't jut out too far for the climber to obtain his first good hold, the average mountaineer of moderate strength and skill may proceed without too much ado. It is helpful, of course, if the steps beneath the overhang are good, as this will give an invaluable assist while the hands are moving up above and as the body is beginning to snake its way around the outer edge.

Many overhangs lack either good handholds above, satisfactory footholds underneath, or project so far as to throw the climber completely off balance. Such climbing becomes either a tour de force of strength and agility, a piece of acrobatics, or is accomplished by strategically pounding a piton in the cliff so that a sling may be placed in it, thus providing an intermediary step. This is artificial climbing, but if the overhang cannot *safely* be forced in other fashion, pride should not dictate against the sling's use. (The pity comes when slings are used indiscriminately on climbs that should be within the range of the good climber's skill.)

Climbing down steep rock is usually harder than going up. This derives from two things: the difficulty of seeing holds from above; the tendency to resist working the hands low enough, thus stretching the body awkwardly and inconveniently across the cliff. Whenever possible it is desirable to descend face out or sideways. While this may suffice for moderate rock, severe climbs have to be descended facing inward. The rope leader will come down last and it is important that his descent be protected by good belaying even as was his upward climb.

Rappelling, sometimes called abseiling or roping down, is a method of getting down steep rock or ice quickly. Done well and under control it can be an exhilarating experience, the body becoming, in a sense, a human elevator. The weight of the rope, and its friction around the body, is the braking force, this being controlled by one hand which feeds the rope upwards as required. Normally, for right-handed people, the rope passes under the top of the right thigh from the front, across the chest to the left shoulder, thence down the back to the right hand. Although this may sound complicated, it is, in fact, simple, and after a little practice the descent can be made in swoops and bounds. Rappelling is not intended, however, to be merely an agreeable experience: its raison d'être is safe and quick descent.

To learn, it is wise to be protected by a belay rope from above. For initial practice, select a sloping rather than a perpendicular cliff. It is merely necessary to walk backwards down the rock, feeding the rope around the body with the lower hand, letting the other hand move

Rappelling, traditional method.

lightly down the rope in front. Most inexperienced rappellers make the mistake of using the front rope to "hang on," but this is neither necessary nor desirable. The body should be kept at an angle to the rock and the feet should be kept somewhat apart for balance to prevent swinging from one side to another. Too, the feet must work down steadily as the hand feeds the rope. If the feet are left behind, the climber soon finds himself in a most embarrassing predicament.

Rappelling, with sling seat.

When this traditional method of rappelling has been mastered, the sling system may be tried. While it is more rapid and less rugged on the trouser seat, it requires much more control. Simply, a piece of sling rope is formed into a figure-of-eight and the climber puts a leg through each eye of the eight until he has it high on his thighs. He then puts a carabiner on the sling where it crosses itself, places the rappel rope through the carabiner, (instead of under the thigh), crosses it up his chest, over his shoulder and down the back to the opposite hand. It will be seen that the carabiner thus absorbs the friction previously apportioned to the thigh and trouser seat. As the rope will move through with less friction, however, the descent will be swifter, but, by the same token, must be more controlled. In using this method, it is important to watch the shirt or parka carefully as there is a tendency for it to get drawn into the carabiner by the rope. This is extremely dangerous and has led to fatality, since it is impossible in mid-rappel to extricate the shirt from the binding point between carabiner and rope. Such danger cannot be too strongly emphasized.

Good rope handling is a fine art, and often the last art mastered by the climber. On rock it should always be remembered that loose rope must not be left lying about or, unless impossible to control, permitted to dangle down a cliff. In the former instance it may be stepped on, tripped over, become tangled, or jam when the leader needs it most. Hanging down the cliff it may get caught on rock or shrubbery and be well-nigh irretrievable. These matters seem basic but otherwise competent mountaineers sometimes bog down in this department. The pay-out of rope should always be carefully scrutinized and, if three people are climbing roped on stiff rock where one person must move at a time, the non-belayer should be charged with coiling and recoiling of rope. It may seem an idle chore yet the success of a climb can depend on the rope's being ready at a crucial moment to run freely and without obstruction. It is always possible to detect a truly good rope handler by the seeming ease with which he keeps the rope always well-coiled and neat. It is an important but hard-bought art.

Chapter 8

The Eternal Snows

*By treating the new snow as Izaak Walton
advises the angler to treat the frog he is
impaling, "use him as though you loved
him," we got across without material risk.*
A. F. MUMMERY

THE RELATIVE difficulties of mastering rock technic vs. snow and ice technic may be debatable, but there is small question that constantly changing conditions make snow climbing more unpredictable. Even when rock is treacherously friable, the situation can be quickly gauged and adjusted to, whereas it takes much experience with snow to be able to judge its condition at a glance. Part of this difficulty lies in the unseen, the conditions beneath the snow's surface. How deep is it, for example? How hard is the surface? Has fresh snow had time either to blow off or adhere to previous layers? On what surface does the snow rest, rock or ice? If on a glacier, where are the crevasses? Does the snow bridge them safely or may it give way to a climber's weight? Above all, can the snow avalanche?

To be able to answer these questions, whatever the circumstances, requires a great deal of experience, sometimes several climbing seasons if one's opportunity to study snow is confined to an annual mountaineering vacation. Yet to be justified in leading a rope up a snow mountain, much more than rudimentary knowledge is required. As mentioned earlier, the skier who also mountaineers will have an advantage for he gets exposure to snow conditions in summer as well as winter, although he must realize that summer and winter snow are not necessarily identical. But the man who only mountaineers will have to start from scratch by asking many questions of his early guides, be they experienced friends or hired leaders, and, coupling the answers with his own observations, he must learn to judge when an almost imperceptible sinking in the snow's surface indicates a hidden crevasse, learn to estimate on the way to the summit what the sun will have done to the snow by the time the party is descending, learn to appraise in advance when crampons will be needed for quicker or safer ascent or descent. It is becoming familiar with conditions on the spot, learning how best to cope with them, that provides the quickest route to mastery of the diverse snow conditions to be encountered on even an easy mountain.

Rock-ribbed regions of snow and ice. East face of the Mischabel group in Switzerland. Highest point is the Dom, the Feegletscher in the foreground.

Types of snow have been broken down into categories varying from three to dozens. A distinguished British authority of both summer- and ski-mountaineering has said that the three basic types of snow requiring climbing familiarity are snow hard enough to walk on, snow so soft that the foot sinks in and avalanche snow. Still another authority has divided snow and ice into over two dozen disparate conditions. The obvious moral is that the mountaineer must always be on the alert to learn more about the state of the snow on which he must climb, bringing theory, practice and judgment to as near maximum efficiency as possible so that he may cope safely with whatever the mountain has to offer, which may very well be a quite different situation today than it was yesterday.

Avalanches, of course, are probably the mountain's most deadly peril, representing as they do a condition over which the climber has little or no direct control. While he may learn to judge when avalanche conditions are prevalent, once it has started the avalanche is capable of destroying not only man but forests and villages as well. Even the wind generated by an avalanche can blow down buildings, so that not only is the snow a peril but the immediate vicinity of the fall becomes dangerous.

There are a multitude of causes of avalanches, even a loud noise, in certain situations, being capable of precipitating the snow slide. Generally, however, the avalanche starts when the weight of the snow on the mountainside overcomes the natural adhesion, or when the support of snow below is insufficient to sustain the weight of the snow above. Wet snow will slide on a slope less steep than dry, and because of its weight wet snow is more dangerous, although the movement of neither type of snow may be regarded carelessly. As soon as it comes to rest, wet snow almost instantly freezes, making it virtually impossible for a trapped climber to extricate himself, if, indeed, he has not been crushed. Escape from dry snow may be somewhat easier, provided he is not buried too deep. If caught in an avalanche, it is necessary to try to stay as near the surface as possible. Keeping the head, if possible, toward the upper part of the mountain, the victim should lie on his back, keeping arms and legs moving as when in swimming. Obviously, the nearer the surface he can remain, the better will be any possible chance of saving himself or of being rescued.

Avalanche danger derives not only from the snow but from possible impact of the body with ice and rocks that are being swept away. Rock avalanches also occur, as do landslides or ice avalanches, the last to be especially watched for in or below the icefall of a glacier. Prevention is almost the only cure for the climber and prevention means staying out of the avalanche's potential track. This is not always feasible, as couloirs have to be crossed, for example, and they provide the natural run for snow. When in an avalanche-potent situation, it is wise to move as quickly as possible, for this is a mountaineering condition in which speed takes precedence over almost every other consideration.

Crossing or climbing glaciers is a normal procedure on almost any snow mountain. Glaciers can be easy and pleasant places to walk; they can also be fraught with pitfalls. When traversing glaciers or climbing them, it is best to assume the latter situation to be standard. Chief villain of the glacier is the crevasse, although in the icefall the serac can be equally dangerous if in tottering condition. Very often, however, the climb can bypass the icefall, whereas the trek on the glacier, crevasses or not, is almost surely part of the ascent. Glaciers are really extremely slow-moving rivers of ice. Just as a stream is boisterous where it splashes over and down its rough bed, or placid on the level stretches, so does the glacier reflect the course dictated by the surface over which it moves and the mountain banks that contain it.

Crevasses are of various kinds depending on their relative position, and according to their direction across or up and down the glacier; thus, for instance, marginal, longitudinal, transverse. It should be remembered that crevasses are most prevalent where the glacier bends over and starts down a steeper slope (as in the rapids of a river) or where the glacier turns a corner or meets another glacier. The icefall occurs in the "rapids," and seracs are formed, large blocks or peaks of ice that are enormously dangerous because of their precariousness and weight, the sun and the churning of glacier movement undermining them daily.

Going up a glacier.

More often than not the glacier surface is snow-covered. It is necessary, therefore, to learn to detect hidden crevasses from the surface of the snow. Wherever there is suspicion, visual detection can be supplemented by probing with the ice-ax. If the ax goes in full length without appreciable resistance the climber had best tread forward with suspicious care, being well-belayed from the rear. Sometimes the crevasse will be covered at its middle portion yet quite visible on either side. Again, it may be that only a snowbridge remains across the open crevasse. Use of such snowbridge will depend on its depth, condition of the snow and how treated in crossing. The leader will first probe with his ax. Then, if he feels the bridge will hold, while given a good belay he may tread carefully across. Sometimes he must crawl, distributing his weight thusly across a larger area. The snow-bridge can never be treated as surely sound but must always be approached and used with extreme wariness. It is well to remember that conditions are at their best in the early morning when the air is cold and at their worst when the sun is beating down.

If the climber feels himself falling into a crevasse, he should try to do two things simultaneously. First, he should give immediate warning to the other member or members of his party so that a belay can be taken at once, or better secured if already belayed. Second, if possible he should throw himself forward toward the far edge of the

On the glacier.

crevasse, jamming the pick of his ice-ax into the snow ahead of him. If the crevasse is not too wide, and if only one leg has gone through, this manoeuvre may save him, though it must be an instinctive act as gravity acts without reflex time.

A condition similar to that of the crevasse, but one that generally can be anticipated, exists at the bergschrund, the separation between the snow adhering to the lower reaches of the mountain and the glacial field below it. The upper lip of the crevasse formed here is usually higher, sometimes considerably so. If a snowbridge cannot be found, the leader must cut his way down the lower lip and up the wall of the higher. Bergschrunds make for difficult mountaineering and, lacking a bridge on or near the surface, must be attacked where the extremities of the lips are not too severe.

Skirting a crevasse.

If the icefall is to be threaded, two dangers must be guarded against: losing the way; fall of seracs. Route-finding in an icefall of any size can be quite difficult, particularly before daylight or in adverse weather. If it has been possible to sight the route in advance from above, some difficulty may be avoided. To avoid serac danger, it is necessary to get through early in the day. It may be possible to circumvent part or all of an icefall by clinging to the rocks or moraine at its side. If such alternative is feasible, it should be considered the route of choice.

The glacial moraine is the heap of rock and rubble that borders the glacier or lies heaped up at its foot. There is no particular problem of crossing a moraine or of walking up it except that the stones may be loose and make uncomfortable going. Occasionally the moraine obtrudes upon the glacier and guard must be taken against stones and rubble that obscure crevasses. In the icefall, if patches of silt and stones cover the surface, it should be assumed that there is danger and the suspicious area avoided.

Cornices are wind-formed wave-like crests adorning snow ridges and vary in size from a few inches to many feet. They are one of the mountain's secret weapons. From the windward side their detection is difficult, yet they must be completely avoided as they can break off without warning if weight comes upon them. The route up a corniced ridge must be well away from the edge. It is much better, even though more difficult, to cut across the top of a steep slope than to walk within the cornice's fracture point. Conversely, it is foolish to walk under a cornice if such route may be avoided, as a falling cornice is as dangerous as rock and may even start an avalanche. Occasionally a double cornice will be encountered, in which the wave-like overlap is first one way, then the other. Unless there is a safe bypass, such route will have to be abandoned.

A party is usually able to move together when snow-climbing unless a pitch is so steep as to make step-cutting necessary. Rope-handling, therefore, is somewhat different than on rock. As the rope should not drag unnecessarily in the snow, and as it is necessary to allow for changes of pace of each climber under varying conditions, the second and third on the rope will each carry two or three coils in one hand. The leader may do this, too, although where crevasses are prevalent it is better for him not to have slack rope as this would only lengthen a fall. The looped coils may be taken up or let out as necessary while the party is in motion. Among crevasses, however, there should be at least 30 feet of rope between each member of the party. It has been seen that a party of two is nearly ideal on rock, but on a glacier three is better, not only for the added protection but for possible crevasse rescue.

When crevasses converge on the route, it is often best for the leader to move alone while provided with a belay around an ice-ax by his second. After he has crossed the dubious bit, or jumped a narrow crevasse, the next member of the party may proceed, protected or not as the leader may have found wise. Belay protection will always be provided wherever snow conditions, steepness or ice make it desirable that the party move one at a time. When moving together, each member of the rope must be ready to provide a quick belay if a slip should occur, and it is important that there be enough rope available to allow the belay to be taken before the next climber be pulled from his tracks.

Once a climber has had the misfortune to fall into a crevasse and is hanging free, the principal danger is that the rope pulling against his chest will constrict his breathing and rapidly bring about unconsciousness. To guard against this, it is wise, especially if the rope is only a two-man team, for each to tie himself in about five feet from the rope's end. At the end of the spare length an overhand loop can be made that will hang just to the ground so that it could be stepped in. While climbing, this loop is worn hanging through the waist rope. If there is a fall, it can be quickly freed and the victim can step in this loop, thus relieving at once the strangling pressure of the rope around his chest. It is also possible for the climber to have prusik slings attached to his rope in advance, knots which will slide up the rope when no pressure is on them, but which provide support immediately there is weight. This technic of climbing a rope via prusik knots can help the crevassed-climber to rescue himself, although prusik technic must be learned in advance, not at time of emergency.

On snow and ice, the ice-ax is second only to the rope as an adjunct to climbing. Not only can it be used for probing crevasses, it is used for cutting steps, clearing steps, for direct aid on steep slopes, for balance, for belaying, and sometimes for support, although its use as a cane is not considered good form.

Step-cutting is an art. While anybody can cut steps in snow slopes, not everybody can cut good steps, steps that are adequate to the circumstance, large enough yet not too large, made with minimum effort for maximum effectiveness. The best way to learn to cut good steps is to receive instruction on a glacier, preferably among some safe seracs.

Steps should be cut so that they slope slightly inward and their surface should be reasonably level, although small snow and ice chips will help rather than hinder forming the step when it is stepped in, congealing from pressure. On a very steep slope it is better to cut upwards in a fairly direct line, cutting handholds if necessary. The

Cutting steps.

handhold on a steep ascent will be essential to the leader as well as an assist to those who follow, although such holds are a time- and energy-consuming luxury if cut when not absolutely needed. If steps are required on a slope of moderate pitch, the route is usually made diagonally, zigzagging back and forth. At turns, the outer step should be made large enough for the climber to change step as he changes direction.

There is no way to master step-cutting except practice. Cutting a route up is simpler than cutting down, as in the latter case the step-cutter must lean outward and down to fashion the step. Two hands may be used on the ax whenever balance permits, although whether one-handed or two-handed cutting is in order, the swing should be moderate, the weight of the ax being allowed to do the work. A supple wrist is excellent equipment for step-cutting.

Whether going up or down, care must be taken not to cut steps so closely above one another that the upper may give way from being undercut. Steps cut too far apart are also the plague of climbers with shorter stride than the leader's, so all consideration must be given to the needs of those who follow. It has been suggested that it is possible to practice cutting steps downward in the kitchen. The system recommended is to stand with one foot on the chair and one on a front rung, facing outward. Imagining a point near the floor, the ice-ax is then swung at that point and stopped there in a steady chopping motion. This may have some slight value as off-snow practice, provided the chair is not toppled forward in the process, precipitating a curious kind of climbing accident!

In ascending a steep snow slope, the ice-ax shaft can be thrust into the snow and used as a hand-hold. It is best, however, not to hoist the body up by this method, the legs, as in rock climbing, being the means of ascent, the ax being used for balance and perhaps a slight pull. In traversing a steep slope, the ax is held across the body with the point pressing repeatedly against the upper side of the slope. This gives a nice sense of balance and is most reassuring, as the body must be held upright and not lean into the mountainside. Too, in crossing a narrow ridge of snow, the ax can be used very gently in front to give a third point of contact (but not of support) which can be comforting where slopes drop off sharply on either side.

In case of a slip, the climber falling should hold his ax in front of him, vertically to his body, digging the point into the snow and pressing with all possible force. If applied quickly, this method may arrest a fall on a snow slope, and will appreciably help the belayer by reducing the shock on him if the rope pays out full length.

On ice, of course, all of the above procedures are more delicate. Cutting ice steps, for example, is a finer process, great care being re-

Crampons preclude slipping and make it possible to cut smaller steps.

quired to avoid breaking the ice away in large pieces. Steps will be smaller and must be more nicely used for ice is generally brittle. Progress across brittle ice, or thin-layered ice on rock, is precarious business and ought only be tackled by experts, for the dangers are considerable, a slip on a steep ice slope being almost impossible to arrest.

On hard snow or ice, it is well to use crampons. By biting into the surface, crampons make progress possible where boots would be inadequate, even if nailed. On many slopes crampons render step-cutting unnecessary, thus appreciably speeding the climb. Too, on a steep pitch where steps have been cut, crampons will assure safe use of the step, and they are invaluable to the leader who must stand in his own steps as he cuts more above. Too, on very small steps, as in ice climbing, it is possible to bite with only two points of a crampon, making a pitch possible that might not otherwise be climbed.

Walking and climbing in crampons requires some practice but facility can be acquired easily. On the normal slope, it is necessary to place all points of the crampon into the snow or ice at once and to

Putting on crampons.

stand with the weight bearing directly downward, not leaning out or in. This requires a flexible ankle but is a much easier technic than initial clumsiness may indicate. In walking, care must be taken to pass the feet a little wider than ordinarily lest a point of the crampon catch the boot, bootlace, sock, trouser or rope. In coming down snow slopes, the crampon will bite the snow well, making rapid progress possible. If the snow is wet, however, it may ball up between the points and make the descent slippery. Kicking each heel sharply into the snow with each step may dislodge such snow, or occasional taps of the bootedge with the ice-ax will serve that purpose. If the snow continues to ball badly, however, it may be wise to remove the crampons unless they will be needed again shortly. In lacing the crampons, they should fit firmly yet not so tightly that circulation will be restricted, as under severe conditions this could lead to frostbite.

Crampons may not be needed if it is possible to kick steps in the snow. If each foot as it moves up makes a small backward arc, then swings sharply into the slope, good steps can be made if the snow is of right consistency. Each person following should use precisely the

Long-pointed and short-pointed crampons. Each is effective; the latter are lighter, and also easier when snow and rock alternate.

same step, enlarging it no more than can be helped. Descending, the heel should be driven sharply into the snow with each step. If carefully and steadily done, the descent may thus be accomplished with considerable rapidity, in some cases almost at a run. It is essential that steps not be unnecessarily enlarged or fallen into as this will make them ineffective, if not dangerous, for those who follow. The technic is to lean slightly forward keeping the weight directly over the feet and using the ax lightly in passing. Even under good conditions, however, it may be desirable for the leader (who, of course, descends last) to wear crampons as he would then be better able to hold a slip.

The body's relationship to the slope cannot be reemphasized too much. It should be kept upright with the weight always directly above the feet regardless of the inclination of the slope. Any disposition to lean forward into the slope going up, or backward coming down, must be resisted. In traversing, the same holds true. The temptation to cling to the mountain is universal and normal, but to yield is not only bad form, it may bring on an accident or, at best, spoil the steps in which others have to climb.

Unlike rock climbing, the hands are not used as direct adjuncts on snow or ice unless the climb is extremely steep. The ice-ax occupies one hand, several coils of rope the other. Freezing temperatures are not conducive to use of the hands, even when gloved. When the gloves get wet or frozen, it is an open question whether the hands are colder with or without them. But on those pitches where holds are provided for the hands, they may be used as in rock climbing, for balance and security, although no hold should be lingered at lest the fingers become numb and thus useless through lack of touch.

Climbing long snow slopes can be enormously tiring for the legs. It is essential that a rhythmic pace be struck early and that that pace be slow enough to allow for ample reserve. The steadiness of even the slowest pace will be faster than a rush and stop, rush and stop technic. If the snow has good consistency, the climb will be less fatiguing for the legs than if the steps sink in to the ankle, calf or knee. An early start is the best safeguard against being on the mountain when the snow has deteriorated to this bad condition. In descending, the knees should be kept slightly flexed to reduce the repeated shock of the body's weight. Where it is possible to rush down with sharp thrusts of the heel, however, the leg will have to be almost rigid.

Resting in steps.

If a high order of difficulty is encountered, hardware may be used. Since only the most experienced climbers should engage slopes requiring pitons and carabiners, it need only be stated here that the general purpose and technic of using hardware is the same as on rock: the leader must be safeguarded, the pitons soundly placed. Ice pitons are carefully driven in and allowed to freeze in place. This doesn't take much more time than driving a piton in a rock crevice except that care must be taken not to make too large a hole by breaking away ice in the vicinity of the piton. Some piton hammers have a pointed as well as a blunt end, the point being useful in starting a hole for the piton or in making a small handhold. Carabiners are used exactly as in rock climbing.

Use of ice piton. (Courtesy Swiss National Travel Office.)

Glissading is the technic of skiing down a mountainside on one's boots, using the ice-ax as a braking force to control speed and help maintain balance. *Glissading must never be indulged in when the conditions below are unknown.* Quite a speed is possible when coming down a mountain in this fashion but the descent must be completely under control. If a bergschrund impends, if crevasses are present, if rocks break the snow's surface or are only thinly hidden, glissading can be fatally dangerous.

One method is simply to stand as when skiing, to turn as when skiing, to stop as when skiing. Another is to bend down, holding the shaft of the ax under the arm, the head held by the opposite hand across the body, the near hand holding the shaft low and behind, controlling speed by pressing down in the snow or by releasing. There is even the well-known *sitz*-glissade for the novice or the weary, although this is a wet, bumpy procedure that will be resorted to only when the legs are too fatigued to cope with the strain of the ordinary glissade.

As has been intimated, belaying is as essential a technic as can be learned and it will be wise to spend an afternoon early in each vacation on easy slopes fielding one's friends, and being fielded, to get the touch of ice-ax, rope and belay when the ultimate strain comes. If the ax is pressed well into the snow with as much as possible of the belayer's weight on it and if the feet are well braced, a hard fall may be sustained. Or if it is practical to lean one leg against the lower side of the thrust-in ax, additional support can be gained, and this may be necessary when the snow is shallow, too hard, or on ice. The trick, of course, is to be ready and able to strike a good belay on a moment's notice in time of crisis. To have plenty of time to fix a belay for those following, or for the leader when the party is moving one at a time, gives room for reflection and selection. It is the finished climber who, by speedy action, saves a fall, giving the impression of prescient anticipation.

As in all phases of mountaineering, on snow and ice judgment of the probable safety of the climb rests with the leader. He must be able to estimate the length of the climb, allowing for an early enough start, over all remonstrances, to permit finishing, which means being off the mountain, before sun or changeable weather has deteriorated snow conditions so badly as to make the climb unsafe. He must know at a glance if there is avalanche danger. He must instantly recognize those situations in which speed is essential. He must know whether the capabilities of his party will meet the test of a traverse across an ice slope. He must be alert to fatigue in others and adjust the pace accordingly, even calling retreat if the physical condition of a member of his rope has deteriorated to the point wherein safety of the party may be jeopardized.

Leading a party on a snow and ice climb is a great responsibility. It can also be a memorable pleasure if ability and prudence go hand in hand.

Chapter 9

The V.I.P.

And back against the rock he bore
And firmly placed his foot before: —
"Come one, come all! This rock shall fly
From its firm base as soon as I!"
SIR WALTER SCOTT

IT IS COMMONLY supposed that the leader is number one man on the rope in all senses. While he is the "captain," so to speak, whose wishes must be quickly and willingly obeyed, and while he has the burden inevitably befalling the "first on the rope", any leader worthy the name would readily concede that there is an equally important position, one that is sometimes lost sight of yet which can be responsible for the success, and even the life, of a climbing party. That very important personage is the second, the belayer, the one who stands ready to protect the leader in the unhappy circumstance of such need arising.

So crucial is the task of the belayer that there has even developed the term "psychological belay". This is a confidence and ability that enables a climber to approach and solve problems because he knows that he is well-belayed that he would not think of attempting with a poor second or an inadequate belay. This facility must not be misconstrued as indicating foolhardiness or disregard of safe climbing procedure. It is rather to be understood as an indication of the true worth of the good second on the rope. The rope itself is a sort of wireless along which run messages between climbers. Just as a sensitive mountaineer can detect almost sight unseen any difficulty along the rope, so can he climb with added confidence and enjoyment when the message is transmitted that all is well.

For purpose of definition, belaying can be considered as that protection one climber affords another by taking in the rope or paying

Tying in to piton and carabiner.

The tie-in.

Sitting waist belay.

it out around his body as the other person moves. Should a fall occur, the weight would be taken by the body and a severe fall slowed to a standstill by the combination of the rope's friction around the body and the control of the hands. While this seems reasonably straightforward, it may suffer from oversimplification. Consider the simplest belay first.

In this method, the leader is belaying from a sitting or standing position *above* the second man. As this second (or third) climbs, the

Standing waist belay.

leader steadily takes in the rope around his waist, leaving only enough slack to prevent the climber from feeling that he is being pulled up. (The constant tug at the waist by a poor belayer can be most exasperating and disruptive of morale.) Thus, if the climber fell, he could not go far for there would not be much slack. A few inches or a foot might be maximum, plus whatever the rope might stretch. If the leader has placed himself carefully, there should be no untoward result from

Standing shoulder belay (the weakest method of belaying).

such a slip. However, should the climber be off to one side, as when the route traverses a cliff, there would be some swing, but under average conditions the fall should still be controllable for the good leader will have considered the difficulties inherent in such a traverse. If the second man is belaying the third climber, the principle remains constant. There should be no danger to the party as a whole because the slip or fall should be minor. It is not so much the weight of a climber that makes a fall difficult to hold as the force. Thus, a light climber falling a given number of feet can be as hard to hold as a heavier person falling a shorter distance.

In this discussion of belaying, wherein the possibility of falling is discussed freely, the idea must not be gleaned that falls in climbing are common. They are, indeed, few in number among average climbers, and among experienced climbers almost non-existent. It has been well said that the mountaineer is in much more danger driving to and from the cliffs than he is when happily employed scampering through the crags.

The difficulty to be considered, then, the one that hopefully will remain in the field of theory rather than practice, is how to arrest a leader fall. A number of circumstances come into play, all of which, or any one of which, may be decisive at a moment of crisis. First, for example, there is the belayer's position. There are two alternatives in most belay spots except the thinnest: the belayer is sitting or he is standing, the latter most assuredly when the belay stance is thin. Theories vary as to which position is safer, some climbers liking the standing belay as being stronger, others the sitting. Whichever the method of choice, on rock of any difficulty the belayer will have secured himself to a tree, to a sturdy rock, or to a well-placed piton and carabiner. The rope to this tie-in should be just barely taut and should not be primarily relied on for the belay, being, rather, a safe-guard, a form of insurance.

When the belayer is well-secured, and when he has the rope passing around his waist and paying out in the direction of the leader, the latter may proceed. As the leader climbs, the belayer will feed out the rope, not permitting much slack to accrue, but neither keeping the rope taut enough to be bothersome. The second must be alert to take in the rope again if the leader retreats or changes direction, and he must be prepared to pay it out at varying speeds according to the leader's progress.

Let it be supposed that a leader has climbed fifteen feet above his belayer and that he has not yet passed the rope through a carabiner. What would happen if he now fell? Unless the belay ledge be unusually large, in which event the belayer could afford no protection other than to keep the falling man from rolling off, the fall would be thirty feet, or twice the distance the climber was above the ledge when he slipped. According to the most elementary physics formula, the total elapsed time of this free fall would be only one and 37-100ths seconds. As-suming that the leader had warned he was about to fall, which is not inevitably the case, the second on the rope has less than two seconds to (a) realize that a fall is imminent or happening, (b) weigh the consequences to the leader, (c) weigh the consequences to himself, (d) weigh the consequences to others on the rope, (e) plan how best to check the fall, (f) brace himself to receive the shock, (g) take the full effect of the fall. Granted that some of these considerations will overlap or transpire simultaneously, and granted that the good belayer will have some conception of how best to stop a fall and will have automatically gauged in advance the potential of the situation, *the elapsed time is still less than two seconds*. Scarcely enough time to pray.

A number of experienced climbers have given much consideration so this problem. Some climbing groups train beginners with various forms of "belay testers," devices in which heavy weights to simulate a body are released through a given fall so that the climber may test himself by stopping them, thus graphically illustrating in advance what impact to expect. This is good, although the experience in stopping a falling body cannot be fully realized until lived through. Test conditions are nonetheless desirable, although all practice falls have the advantage of the expected, a condition which is not ordinarily the case when a fall occurs on the mountain.

Since due to the speed of the fall the climber's full weight can come on the rope with incredible swiftness, almost inevitably the standing belayer will be brought to his knees and strain will come on his tie-in. This should underscore the necessity of tying-in most carefully when preparing to belay. Another imponderable is the ability of the hands to absorb much running of the rope. Heat will be generated quickly and the body must be allowed to absorb as much of such energy as possible. Gloves are sometimes worn by belayers, but their use is debatable and can stimulate argument between climbers of similar background and capability. The advantage of the gloveless hand is that the fingers and palms can be more sensitive to the rope and thus handle it better, although damage to palms and fingers in holding a fall can be serious.

Most discussed among methods of controlling free leader falls is the "dynamic belay", sometimes also spoken of as the "running belay". It is basic that when a heavy fall occurs the belayer cannot arrest it at once, some slippage of the rope through his hands inevitably taking place. The principle of the dynamic belay is to capitalize on such slippage *by letting it happen*. It is then conceived as possible that the belayer can bring the falling climber to rest by slowing the rope to a stop rather than by attempting an instantaneous halt. It is further suggested that it is both possible and desirable to stop the fall within a given distance, that distance being approximately equal to one-third of the distance fallen. Thus, in the example given above, in which the leader presumably falls thirty feet, it is assumed and expected that within a rope run of ten feet after impact the fall may be checked. This adds up to a total descent of forty feet. Not completely incidental is an extra thought process for the belayer to cope with at time of the accident.

Since in such a fall there will inevitably be rope run, it being almost impossible for anybody to stop such a fall without slippage, the theory of the dynamic belay has a good basis. Whether or not, however, under other than laboratory conditions, a mathematical formula can be brought to bear that will be determining is a moot question. To expect the belayer to appraise the situation at each moment and to have a readily worked out decision prepared if a fall should take place, or to expect him to be able to make such careful and precise judgment at the instant of acute crisis, is expecting too much. Almost surely, the belayer is going to stop a fall as quickly and capably as he possibly can. This is the fact, however acceptable the theory. Formulas are all very well, but in the final analysis the fate of the climber will depend on how much the body can take. This applies particularly to the one falling, for there are limits beyond which his body will yield to the impact, causing severe internal injuries, even if outwardly he escapes unscathed. Certainly a slow stop will lessen the damage to the falling climber, but to time the dynamic belay so as to lessen the shock of coming on the rope when the maximum free fall has been reached is to expect incredibly split-second timing.

A different situation prevails when the leader has passed his rope through a carabiner and is climbing to one side of it or above it. In such case, the fall would be the distance beyond the carabiner multiplied by two. Thus, a fall six feet above the carabiner-piton would become a fall of twelve feet. The maximum strain then would come on the piton and carabiner rather than on the belayer. If the piton has been carefully placed, and is in good condition (not rusted), it may be expected to withstand such a fall. Should it come out of the cliff as a result of the impact, it may well have slowed the fall sufficiently to help the belayer when the problem becomes his, as it would do directly.

Belaying on snow climbs presents problems of a different sort. There the ice-ax is used as the point of belay and the rope is passed around it, the ax being driven firmly into the snow, the belayer's weight leaning on the ax and the feet being as securely braced as possible.

Leader belayed through a carabiner as he rounds a corner.

If a fall occurs while the party is moving together, a good mountaineer can quickly appraise the situation, thrust his ax into the snow, whip the rope around it and hold. Since the fall will usually be slower than on a rock face, unless it be into a crevasse, in which event it can be startlingly sudden, there is a slight time balance in favor of the belayer. In recent years there have been two spectacularly successful belays of this sort. On South America's Yerupaja, for example, Maxwell fielded Harrah after the latter had fallen 125 feet. This incredible stop was later surpassed by Schoening's arrest of the fall of a complete party on the descent of K2 in 1953. If more graphic evidence of the necessity of successful belaying were necessary, it would be hard to come by.

All possible mountaineering contingencies cannot, of course, be conjured up, but if the second on the rope be continuously aware of the importance and significance of his position, if he will fully accept the responsibility, if he will remain alert, cool and ready for each changing possibility, he will earn the respected title of most important man on the rope.

chapter 10

He Who Goes First

See that ye walk circumspectly.
ST. PAUL

To STRIKE a paraphrase from Shakespeare's "Twelfth Night", "Some are born leaders, some achieve leadership, and some have leadership thrust upon 'em." As in all walks of life, in climbing there are degrees of talent, proficiency and aptitude, but more than in most activities it is essential to know where leadership ability lies. Woe to those who "have leadership thrust upon 'em" before they are ready to cope with it!

Anybody with physical facility and a taste for the mountains may become a passable climber. There are many joys in the hills for this person, and the snowfields and crags are accessible within reasonable limits. Whether, however, he can become a sufficiently dexterous mountaineer to warrant his going first on the rope is a much more serious question. Unless he be one of the few "born leaders", he will have to achieve leadership, and in such achievement there are a number of imponderables.

It is natural to assume that rope leadership depends on developing enough technical dexterity and know-how to be able to climb safely and well, to be able to find the route, handle the rope, and be ready and able to control a slip or fall. Each of these is a facet of the total requirement of leadership, but there remains another essential, a not easily definable quality, that must be part of the leader's total equipment, an asset no leader can be without. That quality is good judgment.

Webster's Unabridged Dictionary has this to say about judgment: "The operation of the mind, involving comparison and discrimination, by which knowledge of values and relations is mentally formulated". Or further, "The power of arriving at a wise decision or conclusion on the basis of indications and probabilities, when the facts are not clearly

Setting up a belay.

ascertained". Each of these definitions has validity as a possible yard-stick by which judgment may be measured, but knowledge of the requirements will not suffice. More than any other demand upon the climber, judgment must be an innate quality brought to the sport.

The greatest test of the climber's judgment is his willingness to turn back. If he has an off day, he should recognize this at once and forsake the climb. If the weather turns against him, if time is running out, if a weak member of the party imperils safety and success, in face of any one of a multitude of such "if's" the leader must be able to give the signal for retreat. He may be met with chagrin, disappointment, perhaps even scorn, but if his knowledge and instinct dictate "Tomor-row, not today", his decision should be made readily and cheerfully, in face of whatever obstacle. It is not easy to disappoint one's friends, much less oneself, but there must be no equivocation: if this is not the day, the climb must be abandoned. It is frustrating to have to turn back on the Matterhorn with the summit in sight, but it is better than to have attained the crest without living to tell about it.

Judgment involves many things: weather, conditions on the moun-tain, ability of the composite rope of climbers, form, safety, time,

"On belay!"

"hunch". The climber who can recognize *and acknowledge* his own varying capacity is one blessed with the seeds of good judgment. He very likely will become a reliable leader more quickly than a flashier mountaineer whose virtuosity outmatches his wisdom.

Included in judgment is the ability to appraise the members of the climbing team, to use them for maximum effectiveness, to deploy them so that the rope is always at its best climbing strength. For ex-

Face climbing. Body is vertical.

ample, if a delicate traverse is to be made horizontally across a cliff, a weak member of a three-man party should be placed in the middle so as to have equal protection by a belay in front and to the rear. While this is an elementary tactic, it is the kind of decision that the leader will make automatically.

The leader's responsibility cannot be minimized. The welfare of each person climbing behind him on the rope is his direct charge. He can never be ruffled, uncertain, indecisive, faltering — or, if he is, he must not let his hesitancy be evident to those on his rope. This does not mean that he may not acknowledge mistakes. If in error, it is far better for him to admit the matter at once, rectify the mistake and take up from there. More respect by far will be earned from an error admitted than from a mistake muddled through.

The technics of rope leadership are, in essence, simply the technics of good mountaineering. Among other things, the leader should be a teacher, with a teacher's patience, for it is frequently necessary to demonstrate methods to the less adept. It would be a poor leader of a climb who could not be lavish with patience, whether it be waiting for good weather or waiting for a slowpoke. A mountainside is as poor a place as there could be for quick temper, although this danger must be guarded against, as altitude plays strange tricks on the mind, making many men curt and irritable. An imperturbable good humor up high is a priceless asset, although it does not follow necessarily that the valley humorist is the altitude cut-up. The fact may lie in the opposite direction. The leader, however, must be continually aware of dispositional danger signals in himself as well as in others, since his calm may be needed.

Invariably a good leader is a good follower. If climbing second, for example, the sound leader will instinctively know how to give support to he who goes first on the rope. He will sense when slack rope is required or when the rope should be taut; he will see to it that all rope or ropes are kept in good order; he will be alert to the mood and welfare of others in the party, relieving the leader of much of this concern when the latter is addressing himself to technical problems of the climb. The leader who is seconding will point out how the present leader accomplishes tricky steps, thus helping to arouse another's observation in a useful way; he will keep a relaxed attitude prevalent, even if the going is tense; he will be responsive to the leader's least wish or difficulty. In a very positive sense, the leader as second will be like the understudy in a theatre — ready to go on if emergency arises.

Leadership potential can be detected early. A sure sign is the sense of responsibility a climber, even as a novice, shows to the party with which he is climbing. What are some of these responsibilities? The mountaineer must first, last and always respect his leader, accepting his judgment and word without question. When snap decisions must be made, there is no room for debate. If the rope consists of three climbers, the third must also give full cooperation to the second man,

Ascending snowfield.

providing him with a back belay if that would be helpful, seeing that the rope is coiled or recoiled so that it will pay out well, accepting the second as the leader's alter ego when the latter is farther ahead, particularly if out of easy communication. The third man also owes himself a responsibility, it being paramount that he climb as safely as consistent with his ability, with a continued awareness of his form or lack of it and of his ability to meet the problem in hand. In the mountains it is always better to discard pride and acknowledge difficulty, as false pride goeth before a fall. Again, each climber has a responsibility to the sport. Mountaineering is sometimes dangerous and its stature and pleasures are best safeguarded by safe climbing. An irresponsible climber can mar the sport for others by his exhibitionistic tendencies, his monkey tricks, his steeplejacking, his dangerously spectacular feats, his death. Such a one shows none of the traits that make for leadership in the mountains, or in life for that matter, since in the hills, as in life, the best leadership is innate, not imposed.

It is important that leaders, or all climbers, be able to recognize the difficulty of a climb. In rock work a code has been devised that gives a sense of what can be expected, a common denominator, variable, perhaps, but at least a guide. The code runs approximately like this. Walking along the level in unimpeded fashion might be called Grade 1. Walking uphill would be Grade 2 if the ascent be moderate, while a steep hillside, trail climb or rockfall would be rated 3. In stiffer climbing than this, the grades would range from 4 to 6. Thus a Grade 4 climb would require use of the hands, and Grade 5 would be getting into stiff rock work when mountain boots start to feel clumsy. Artificial aid, either slings or rope tension, would be the measure of a Grade 6 climb. Sometimes in-between gradations are used, as 3½ or 5½, or a "low four" or a "strong five". Any such modifications, naturally, would vary with the individual, chimneys being poison to one climber, faces to another. These numerical gradings, once related to climbs, can be extremely useful as an indication of the difficulties to be tackled.

Since an international climbing code has not been established, desirable as such code might be, ratings of climbs vary geographically. In England, for instance, climbs may be called Easy, Difficult, Very Difficult, Severe, Very Severe. Even these vary, however, within the British Isles. Some attempts have been made in the United States to codify climbing procedures, rules and vocabulary, but the sport's individualism has resisted conformity. In certain matters affecting safety, however, it would be desirable for regionalism to be sacrificed and common ground determined.

All leaders should be familiar with the International Distress Signal. It consists of six loud sounds, any kind, at ten-second intervals, a minute's pause and then repeated, the process to be continued until the call is answered by three of any loud sound at twenty-second intervals in alternate minutes. Three of anything is sometimes used in the United States, the response being two of anything. If visibility is possible, smoke signals, blinkers, flag waving, any of these or similar calls for help may be used in the same time pattern.

Leadership ability being an intangible asset, no formula can be prescribed. Just as no party is better than its weakest man, so can it be said that no party can exceed its leader. Judgment first, technic second, may seem like putting the cart before the horse, but reflection will show the dangers inherent in the reverse statement. Lucky is the mountaineer who has both virtues in equal proportion. He may well become one of the mountain greats, provided a generous share of each be his portion.

To achieve leadership there is probably no better advice to offer than was once given by an expert woman climber to a promising yet struggling beginner. *"Always* climb," she said, "as though you are leading."

chapter 11

The Shadowy Line

*The line which separates the difficult from the danger-
ous is sometimes very shadowy, but it is not an imagin-
ary line. It is a true line, without breadth. It is often
easy to pass, and very hard to see. It is sometimes
passed unconsciously, and the consciousness that it has
been passed is felt too late. If the doubtful line is passed
consciously, deliberately, one passes from doing that
which is justifiable, to doing that which is unjustifiable.*

EDWARD WHYMPER

THIS CANNY advice by the conqueror of the Matterhorn possesses the
clue to safe climbing. Because the division between safe climbing and
unsafe is nebulous, it is necessary to be always on guard lest it be
crossed and no line of retreat be found. A climber may justify to
himself the taking of a calculated risk, a chance, a gamble, although it
is questionable whether his sense of individual responsibility, or his
responsibility to the sport, can find such justification, but he can never
knowingly cross Whymper's aptly-titled "shadowy line" if he considers
his duty to the other climbers on his rope. As a leader, he would be
flouting all the qualities that have made leadership available to him.
He would be jeopardizing the welfare (which in climbing can mean
the lives) of his companions, of those who have faith in his common
sense and good judgment. Unless it be to extricate the party from a
hazardous dilemma, the leader can never assume such risk.

Lamentably, mountaineering annals are full of tales of catastro-
phe. Accidents do happen in the mountains, however much climbers
would like to ignore the fact. There are broken limbs and tragically
unnecessary deaths and there always will be. But this is no more a
reason for men to desist from climbing than the latest plane crash is
a call to stop flying, or the latest grisly highway smashup reason to

abolish autos. Accidents are the exception, not the rule, and statistics are more in favor of the climber than of the people in the family car on a holiday weekend.

The important effort that must continually be made in mountaineering is to control the factors that precipitate accidents. This means starting with the individual. It means educating the climber from his novitiate onward into sound mountaineering practice, impressing upon him that it is better to so climb today that he will be able to continue climbing tomorrow, next week, next year. Any lesser standard may lead to misfortune on some climb that will spoil or stop short the pursuit of an otherwise promising career in the hills.

Various analyses of climbing accidents have been made by mountaineering groups, the best being the Accident Report of the American Alpine Club. The AAC's safety committee compiles a list of mountaineering accidents, examines the findings and breaks them down into categories. Year after year it has been found that almost all accidents occur to climbers who are pursuing the sport under uncontrolled circumstances.

"Uncontrolled circumstances" simply means somebody being somewhere on a mountain or a cliff that he shouldn't be. It may be a case of a non-climber scrambling up an apparently innocuous slope until he passes a point of no return, becomes panicky and falls or is benighted; it may be an over-confident climber scrambling on the lower reaches of the Matterhorn above the Hörnli hut and, being unprepared for the mountain's icy condition, slipping to his death on the glacier far below. (This unhappy event has, indeed, occurred, and may serve as apt commentary on the soubriquet "tourist's route" often associated with this ridge of the mountain.) Such accidents always reflect either a lack of know-how or a lack of judgment, but after the fact there is no use making a distinction. The damage has been done, to the individual and to the sport.

Without question the best way to learn climbing is with an organized club. The AAC reports, and findings of other mountaineering clubs, conclusively show that climbers who learn and continue climbing under organized auspices live long, healthy, safe lives, while the preponderance of accidents befall the climber who prefers to go his own way with one or two others of his ilk, or the casual wanderer who gets himself into difficulties beyond his control. Certainly there can be more sympathy and understanding for this last offender than for the individualists who, at an early date, "pass from doing that which is justifiable, to doing that which is unjustifiable". It is the latter group that unfairly lends to mountaineering the reputation of being risky and foolhardy.

Practically as good as learning climbing with a club, of course, would be learning it by climbing regularly with a sound mountaineer. Under the aegis of a tutor one always learns faster. It is almost certain, however, that this elder statesman will belong to a mountaineering club, for there are very few "soloists" in the climbing fraternity. By virtue of the cooperative nature of the sport, there cannot be. A leader does not want an unknown quantity on his rope, although almost any leader worth the name will lavish patience in abundance on a beginning climber who evinces enthusiasm.

Occasionally there will be the individualist who, as a leader, feels he can take anybody on his rope, such supreme self-confidence does he possess in his own ability. Young climbers would do well to eschew such training, if it can be called training, for the ability to climb a mountain is considerably different than the mere ability to "get up it". To an enthusiast who exclaimed about an impossible-looking pitch, "It goes! It goes!" one of the greatest guides of all time murmured, "Yes, *it* goes, but *I* don't go". This is the sort of wisdom that carries the sound mountaineer into serene old age.

A distinction must be drawn between a weekend's rock climb and the summer mountaineering vacation. In rock climbing, the process of tying-in, whether to a carabiner, a healthy tree or a solid spike of rock at each pitch is normally indulged in and should be consistently practiced. The cliffs are steep, a small slip can be disastrous, and on stiff rock only one person should be climbing at a time. In the mountains, where time is a potent factor, the party generally moves together, and even when they don't, there is not always time or facility for repeated tying and untying. Constant attention is the watchword, for the mere fact of not tying in does not indicate that all is safe. It is merely that the clock must count, for it is essential to get off the mountain before the snow is soft or before the sun has melted ice thus releasing frozen rocks to fall. The technics of the mountain ascent, however, should not modify the requirements of the weekend cliff, for safety is relative to the total aspect of the job in hand.

The rigors of high mountaineering cannot be impressed too strongly upon the novice climber. Youth and enthusiasm can decoy the unwary or the unknowing into foolish risks that may truncate a promising climbing career at its very inception. If, through inattention to dressing properly or through over-sureness that a dangerous bit can be managed without a piton's protection, if through such errors of judgment today's climb becomes the last climb, it would have been better for the enthusiast to have chosen another sport where discretion is at a lower premium.

A short time ago the rock climbers of the New York Chapter of the Appalachian Mountain Club devised a Climber's Code. It is a composite of ideas from many climbing sources and it was published in an accident report of the American Alpine Club as well as in James Ramsey Ullman's stimulating book *The Age of Mountaineering*. In the interests of safe climbing, it is given again here because it seems to be the very quintessence of good advice on the sport.

A Climber's Code

The Ascent. No climb is worth the deliberate risk of life nor should it be judged successful if anyone is foolhardy. A judicious retreat is more admirable than a dangerous victory. Be confident that you can get up *and down.*

Judgment. Be alert to your responsibility to others. Know their abilities and limitations as well as your own. Know the limitations of terrain, weather and equipment. Good judgment means knowing these limits.

Margin of Safety. In the interest of speed, some compromise with safety may be wise, but more is needed than "I almost didn't make it."

Companions. There must be mutual respect for the leader's orders to reflect safety. The essence of safe climbing is companionship and cooperation, not competition. *Never climb solo.*

Equipment. Be sure that it is the best both in type and condition. This includes clothing, food and first aid equipment, as well as climbing gear.

Belaying. Good belaying is the most important skill in safe climbing. A man's life may pass through your hands. Experience will show the value of dynamic technique and that he protects others best who protects himself.

Condition. Physical and mental condition should be adequate to your role as a climber. Hard work requires stamina. If you do not feel you can do it, *don't.* Another day may be better for you.

Climbing Ability. Know and practice good form. This includes party organization, signals, rope handling, body coordination, rappelling, and all the details of rock, snow and ice technic which make an expert mountaineer.

Leadership. Everyone is obligated to exercise leadership by promoting safety and discouraging extremism and spectacularity. Give beginners special attention and suggest they climb with an organized group of conservative tradition.

The life you save will be your own. In mountaineering, pride goes before a fall.

chapter 12

Some Notes on Mountaineering Photography

*Any attempt to express one's personality in a picture
of, say, the Matterhorn, is almost certain to result in
a victory for the Matterhorn.*

C. DOUGLAS MILNER

THERE ARE side pleasures in mountaineering, some of which can be
indulged in even by people who do not aspire to the summit, or by
those climbers whose day for the great routes is done. Geoffrey Winthrop Young has said, "a mountaineer is not only one who climbs
mountains, but anyone who likes to walk, read or think about them".
Within the scope of this very catholic definition there lies joy for many,
whether or not they have ever, or will ever, stand atop the Matterhorn.
(Indeed, that airy spot is becoming so populated that the true mark
of distinction will soon be to be numbered among those who *have not*
stood there.)

From shortly after time began men have gazed at mountains in
awe and wonder. Less than a century ago a drab hunchback from
Breuil, Italy, epitomized that amazement for all time. In the company
of Edward Whymper he had his first glimpse of the Matterhorn. With
tears in his eyes, he fell to his knees, saying, "Oh, beautiful mountains!"
It is not customary in our times to let such naked emotion be seen
by our fellows, but anybody who has ever looked at a mountain with
affection will recognize his kin in pathetic Luc Meynet, one who was
never to stand on a summit but who was nonetheless a mountaineer.

Since it is customary for man to want to perpetuate that which
he admires, descriptions of mountains were written early in history,

and sketches and painting followed. In fact, the first time Whymper went to the Alps it was to sketch but his *affaire* with the Matterhorn took precedence. With the advent of photography, cameras soon were carried into the hills, bulky affairs which, with attendant equipment, made a photographic foray to the heights an expedition. Fortunately for today's photographer, amateur or professional, it is possible to take pictures and still climb light, largely due to the advent of the 35 mm. camera.

Since the professional will want to make the climb for the photography rather than have pictures to embellish the climb in after-months the few comments offered here are directed only to those climbers who take photography less seriously than their mountaineering. The intention is not so much to attempt to improve the climber's pictures as to point out that the camera need not be left behind.

The first problem is type of camera. For the climber to whom photography is secondary, the requisite is a camera of minimum weight and bulk, one that may be carried easily and operated readily. A 35 mm. camera is the obvious choice, the make to be determined by pocketbook, remembering that in general a better camera will take better pictures provided it is used correctly. The lens chosen can be an f3.5 50 mm., as at f8 or less good depth of field will be obtained. If pictures in reduced lighting conditions are desired, an f2.8 or even f2 lens may be selected, but such lenses, being faster, are only of maximum use to the experienced amateur.

Much is spoken of the advantage of interchangeable lenses and mountain photography is certainly adaptable to either the telephoto or wide-angle lens. Interchangeable lenses, however, presuppose more expensive equipment, and telephotos or wide-angle will have more value in the valley than on the climb itself. Obviously the selection made will be determined by considerations of pocketbook, immediate objective and long-range planning. Whatever the choice, however, the camera should be picked for compactness and facility.

If the camera is carried in the rucksack, many fine picture opportunities will be lost. It should not, however, be carried loosely around the neck, or even under the shirt, as this invites banging on rocks or other obstacles. Rather, a pocket should be made inside the parka on the left side as closely under the arm as convenient. Carried here, with the strap around the neck, the camera can be brought out in a jiffy, used, and quickly put away. With practice, much picture taking can be done while climbing without interrupting the progress of the rope. This is essential because it sometimes means pictures need not be sacrificed when time on the climb is of the essence. If the going is tricky, such quick shots are not recommended, but at such times the photographer seldom thinks of his camera anyway.

Such rapid-fire snapshots as suggested presuppose good exposure. Lighting conditions should have been appraised in advance, trying to strike what would seem to be an average for the day. Too, an average distance should have been pre-selected and depth-of-field focusing will help. If the photographer is one who revels in five minutes for every exposure, this technic will never do, but then he will probably be summarily informed that there isn't time on the climb for such photography. Nor is there, for no side pleasure may be allowed to intrude upon safety. The choice must arbitrarily be, take pictures as possible and as speedily as possible, hoping that from the many will come the few good. Actually, if forethought has been given before the climb, the results will probably be gratifying in terms of the number of satisfactory shots.

Besides time, the photographer has another, more insidious, enemy. Altitude will spoil more pictures by far than speedy picture taking lower down. Until one has lived at great heights for a protracted period, the mental processes tend to lag. No matter how much you plan with care and resolve to get the precise focus, the right aperture, the correct shutter speed, time and again at altitude, particularly if fatigue has set in, some aspect of the procedure will have been overlooked or done carelessly. Even during a respite on the climb, or at the summit, when some extra moments may be taken, it is surprising to find later what basics have been neglected. Only an iron will or complete acclimatization will overcome this hazard.

Whether to take color for slides, or black and white, will be a matter of personal predilection. Ideally two cameras would be carried, but this is cumbersome as well as additionally expensive. The decision must be made in advance and technics for the method chosen, particularly as to basic or average exposures for varying conditions, mastered beforehand. There is more margin for error when taking black and white, but the color enthusiast will gladly sacrifice some poor exposures if he can get vivid recreation of his mountain and his climb.

Pictures of mountains from afar tend to get into the post card category. As professionals usually take the post cards, it is well to buy their work for its nominal price, taking one's own pictures from vantage points not normally reached. Whenever possible, take pictures of people on the climb itself. This will give perspective to the route, to the mountain, and be much more meaningful afterwards. A far-off picture of the mountain, however, on which the route can be pointed out will always be useful.

Pictures taken directly up or down are usually not satisfactory. If taking a picture of a rock climber, the photographer's best vantage point is to one side against the cliff face. For spectacular shots a climber against the sky is surefire. Get him on a corner, a ridge, from beneath an overhang, get him rappelling against the blue sky. Both of you will be satisfied.

Patience is needed for the truly great shots. They never give forewarning of their availability and the only thing to do is to be ready the instant the opportunity arises. But waiting on the mountain is next to impossible, hence the advice to be always prepared. Properly to photograph a route on a mountain would mean breaking the climb up into stages. One technic sometimes used is to climb the lower half of the route the first day, taking pictures en route, then returning to the hut or high camp. An early start is made the next day and the climb completed to the summit, the upper half of the mountain being photographed on the descent. Under good conditions, and on routes of only moderate difficulty, this plan can be adopted quite usefully. A highly technical climb will take longer and may require a larger party (perhaps a three-man rope instead of a two).

The answer to the filter question is relatively easy. For color, the skylight filter can be put on and left there. At altitude it should always be used, as it will reduce the overabundance of blues. For black and white the yellow filter at 1½ or 2x should be employed if good cloud rendition is to be achieved. Remember, of course, to adjust exposure accordingly.

An exposure meter may be a great help, although reference to it will not always be easy on the mountain. Again there is the question of where to carry it, particularly as it is a delicate instrument. If the basic exposures for the film chosen are memorized, and if one has checked one's judgment of light conditions against the exposure meter in advance, it is possible to dispense with the meter. Snow conditions make the problem more complex, and if there is time it is wise to bracket the picture by taking shots either side of what seems to be the correct exposure. On snow it is best to point the palm of one hand at the source of brightest light, taking the meter reading from the hand, as this gets best results.

The basic principles of all photography are equally applicable in the mountains. The sun shade should always be used, increased exposure is necessary when the object is side-lighted, interesting shots may be taken contre jour, the angle from which the shot is taken may make or break the picture, film should be developed or processed as quickly as possible after exposure, the camera should be checked for operation and cleanliness before the vacation. The more that is known in advance of the climbing trip about photography and about one's camera, the better will be the average of satisfactory shots.

Not least of the pleasures of mountain photography will be showing the results to one's family and friends. If black and whites are taken, the very best can be enlarged and mounted for home decoration. If color has been the choice, an illustrated lecture can be prepared about the virtues of a mountaineering vacation. Do not, however, inflict upon your friends the bad, or even the poor, shots. They will not be interested, unless ardent photographers themselves, on why a picture didn't succeed. They will want to see the one's over which they can "ooh" and "aah." Give them half an hour of your select slides, leaving them wanting more, rather than bore them with an hour of everything that interests you. Explain the pictures, identify the mountains and the people, but don't give a history of the making of each slide. For your own future photography, it will be well if you have kept a record of exposure whenever possible, but only you and your fellow-addicts care about this. In any slide talk, always leave 'em wanting more.

It is a shame to go to the mountains without a camera. Just as a picture recreates a moment in time, so a good collection of shots of a mountaineering vacation will recreate and recall the pleasures, the woes, the pains, the triumphs that made the expedition memorable. Thusly the trip may project itself well into the later years.

chapter 13

Some Mountain Reading

There is no frigate like a book
To take us lands away . . .
EMILY DICKINSON

MOUNTAINEERS TEND toward the taciturn, not talking freely about their sport, and underplaying their achievements. Perhaps as a release to this quality of deprecation, they have written copiously. In the annals of mountaineering adventure, there are few if any significant exploits that have not been recorded. The English have been notably loquacious, having produced shelves of books about their part in the development of the sport. Not far behind have been the Germans, and the French, too, have made sizeable contributions, particularly making attempts at mountaineering fiction, a type of literary endeavor that has fared only moderately well. In America, a beginning has been made, but a small one to date, James Ramsey Ullman being the only significant recorder and possibly the only American to have attempted the climbing novel. As more young Americans come to the sport, this situation will undoubtedly change.

Most mountaineering books contain bibliographies, some of them lengthy. Too, a good idea of the scope of the field can be gleaned from browsing through the climbing catalogs of bookshops, two of the best being Thomas J. Gaston, Booksellers, London, and the Old Settler Bookshop in Walpole, New Hampshire. The difficulty of most bibliographies of this sort, however, is that they give little or no idea of the content of the work, making the ordering of books a risky business, although reputable booksellers will often exchange a book or give credit for a return. It is a calculated risk, then, not to provide a bibliography, but the brief list that follows is not intended as such. It is, rather, meant to be a guide to some mountaineering reading that has pleased one person with an itch for the hills and is offered in the hope it may please others. To offset the "pig-in-a-poke" quality of bibliographies, brief comments are given on the books suggested. Since preference in any area is always intensely personal, it is not anticipated that every book on the list will please every mountaineer. Guidebooks are omitted as they seem more properly to belong in the ensuing chapter on where to climb.

Armchair mountaineering is an old and respected profession. It is not necessary to be able to breach a bergschrund or tread a knife-like ridge to be able to enjoy the rarefied heights. On the other hand, it is a splendid experience for the mountaineer to be able to follow a climb on a winter's night in the words of a kindred spirit, and still more stirring if he has accomplished the same climb himself. Forward, then, to the armchair!

The Complete Mountaineer, George D. Abraham. Contains much common sense about the sport and compelling accounts of alpine climbing.

Peaks, Passes and Glaciers, edited by John Ball. Articles by early members of the Alpine Club about opening of the Alps.

No Picnic on Mount Kenya, Felice Benuzzi. An escape from a British POW camp in Africa for the sole purpose of scaling Kenya.

Climbing in Britain, J. E. Q. Barford. An inexpensive paperback that is a "best buy."

Nanga Parbat Pilgrimage, Hermann Buhl. Autobiography of the audacious climber who "soloed" Nanga Parbat's summit.

Mountaineering, C. T. Dent. The Badminton Library's famous and humorous contribution to climbing literature.

Ascent of K2, Ardito Desio. Successful ascent of the world's second highest peak.

A History of Mountaineering in the Alps, Claire Eliane Engel. One of the few good accounts of the sport's development in Europe.

On Climbing, Charles Evans. Personalization about the sport by a prominent contemporary.

Kanchenjunga Climbed, Charles Evans. The solution of one of the toughest Himalayan problems.

La Grande Crevasse and *Premier de Cordee* (The Grand Crevasse and First On the Rope), R. Frison-Roche. Two mountaineering novels of more than passing interest.

The Art and Sport of Alpine Photography, Arthur Gardner. Written in the 1920's and now out of print. Much value for the amateur photographer.

Le Cervin, Charles Gos. Detailed history of the Matterhorn. (In French.)

116 INTRODUCTION TO MOUNTAINEERING

Handbook of American Mountaineering, Kenneth Henderson. The American Alpine Club's basic book on the sport. Excellent.

The Killer Mountain, Nanga Parbat, Karl M. Herrligkoffer. The successful yet strange expedition to one of the world's most dangerous mountains.

Annapurna, Maurice Herzog. The French expedition that paced mid-20th century mountaineering. Colored by the author's intense feeling for the sport.

K2, The Savage Mountain, Charles M. Houston and Robert H. Bates. The ill-fated American expedition that helped pave the way for the ultimate Italian victory.

The Conquest of Everest, Sir John Hunt. The feat that electrified the world, carefully told by the expedition's leader.

The Mountain Way, R. L. G. Irving. Easily the best mountain anthology.

The Romance of Mountaineering, R. L. G. Irving. An approach to the sport by one who has loved it well.

Belaying the Leader, Richard M. Leonard and Arnold Wexler. The definitive manual on belaying. Indispensable background material for the serious mountaineer.

Mountain Photography, C. Douglas Milner. The definitive book for the climbing photographer.

Rock For Climbing, C. Douglas Milner. A collection of Milner's splendid rock photography.

My Climbs in the Alps and Caucasus, A. F. Mummery. A classic by one of the early mountain "greats."

South Col, Wilfrid Noyce. Personal account of everyday life on the successful British Everest attempt. A good complement to Hunt's "Conquest."

The Matterhorn, Guido Rey. Another lover of the great peak. Coupled with Gos' "Le Cervin," leaves little more to be said.

The Butcher, The Ascent of Yerupaja, John Sack. The successful trip of some young Americans to a South American toughie.

Face Nord, Saint Loup. A worthy but not well-known French novel.

Men, Women and Mountains, Sir Claud Schuster. Well written, well climbed.

Postscript To Adventure, Sir Claud Schuster. The summing up of a life's mountaineering. Beautifully written.

Wie Die Schweizer Alpen Erobert Wurden, Dr. Max Senger. A definitive history of mountaineering in Switzerland. (In German.)

Knots For Mountaineering, Phil D. Smith. An inexpensive, profusely illustrated manual of useful knots.

A Camera in the Hills, Frank S. Smythe. Fine mountain pictures accompanied by good text and analytical notes.

Climbs in the Canadian Rockies, Frank S. Smythe. The great Everester's trek to Canada's northwest.

Mountaineering, edited by Sydney Spencer. Contributions on all phases of the sport by assorted authorities.

High Adventure, Bob and Ira Spring. Two of America's best climbing photographers put their best work in book form, with running commentary by their wives.

The Playground of Europe, Sir Leslie Stephen. A *must* on the library shelf of every climber. Wisdom, history and a shining wit.

The Ascent of Denali, Hudson Stuck. First ascent of Mount McKinley. Hard to come by but worth finding.

Hours of Exercise in the Alps, John Tyndall. Pioneering by a pioneer.

The Mountain World, Swiss Foundation for Alpine Research. Excellent post-World War II annual. Printed in English since 1953.

The Age of Mountaineering, James Ramsey Ullman. America's preeminent mountaineering writer relates some of the great exploits and comments usefully on the sport.

Banner in the Sky, James Ramsey Ullman. Although intended as a boy's book, this is the best American climbing novel and full of sound mountaineering know-how.

Kingdom of Adventure: Everest, James Ramsey Ullman. A quick way to become familiar with the Everest story.

Tiger of the Snows, "autobiography" of Tenzing of Everest as told to James Ramsey Ullman. A "success story" of the most exciting kind.

The White Tower, James Ramsey Ullman. The second best American climbing novel. (See "Banner in the Sky.")

Among The Alps With Bradford, Bradford Washburn. A book on mountaineering by a boy for boys by one who has since become a prominent American mountaineer.

Scrambles Amongst the Alps, Edward Whymper. Account of the climbing that led to the first ascent of the Matterhorn and the author's description of that fateful climb. Together with Mummery and Stephen, "Scrambles" is one of mountain literature's triumvirate of greats.

Mountain Craft, Geoffrey Winthrop Young. The mountaineer's "bible." Not a book to be dashed through, but to be read and referred to across a lifetime.

Mountains With A Difference, Geoffrey Winthrop Young. The inspiring story of how this great climber refused to let the loss of a leg keep him earthbound.

On High Hills, Geoffrey Winthrop Young. Young is a stylist of the printed page as well as of his hills. Beautiful writing, beautiful reading.

It would be unduly optimistic to hope that the books on this tentative list might meet the approval of all climbers. There are, however, enough of established merit to guarantee many hours of contentment by the fireside when reflecting on peaks climbed or looking ahead to the season to come.

chapter 14

Where To Climb

I believe that the ascent of mountains forms an essential chapter in the complete duty of man, and that it is wrong to leave any district without setting foot on its highest peak.

SIR LESLIE STEPHEN

THE ROPE IS A TEAM. Climbing is a cooperative, not a solitary, effort, except when each member of the climbing rope is individually tackling the problem at hand. So while it's simple to assume that "where to climb" is wherever there are mountains, it is more correct to say that climbing is done wherever there are people to climb with. And "people" almost invariably means organized clubs devoted to the sport.

Thirty years ago a prominent English mountaineer said that any time two or three people with a yen for the mountains had a rope, the best way for them to learn was to go out together and climb. This was reckless advice, comparable perhaps to throwing a non-swimmer in deep water to learn how to swim. He may get out — but also he may drown.

The best, quickest and safest way to learn the art of mountaineering is to climb with a club, with people who know the sport, who have trained others and been so trained themselves. Here will be found climbers of experience, of know-how, of sufficient patience to be willing to spend time instructing the earnest novice. Of course, some clubs are only for the expert, and other clubs are so crowded that they are reluctant to add to their rosters because they cannot always provide for current membership. There isn't a climbing group worthy the name, however, that will turn an eager newcomer away unadvised.

Some of the responsible climbing clubs with which affiliation would be desirable are named below. If you approach one of them, do so with deference to their problems. Do not assume that each new-comer will be welcomed with open arms. The members of such clubs will generally be helpful and, to the best of their ability, cooperative, and most will find a way to introduce you to mountaineering if convinced of your sincerity and adaptability. But be considerate of the fact that climbers do not want to spend all of their sunny days teaching, that they sometimes want to disport themselves on climbs that may be beyond you. If the day comes when you can equal them, or even surpass them, your new-found friends will be as pleased as you and delighted to have you on the cliffs and ridges. And then you, in turn, may share the training of others who are then new to the sport.

From Maine's Katahdin to Washington's Rainier, clubs will be found, even the mid-West's Iowa having an active group. Many colleges and universities have busy clubs, and a few of those are indicated here. But whether you be near the Appalachians, the Rockies, or the ranges of the Pacific Coast, you will find groups of kindred spirits banded together, and it is among such responsible clubs that you will best learn safe and sane mountaineering.

Adirondack Mountain Club	
American Alpine Club	N. Y. C.
Appalachian Mountain Club	Boston
(Chapters throughout New England and in N. Y. C.)	
Canadian Alpine Club	
California Alpine Club	San Francisco
Cascadians	Yakima, Wash.
Chicago Mountaineering Club	
Colorado Mountaineering Club	Denver
Dartmouth Mountaineering Club	Hanover, N. H.
Desert Rats	Richland, Ore.
Federation of Western Outdoor Clubs	Eugene, Ore.
Georgia Appalachian Trail Club	Atlanta
Green Mountain Club	
Harvard Mountaineering Club	Cambridge, Mass.
Hood River Crag Rats	Hood River, Ore.
Inter Mountain Alpine Club	Richland, Wash.
Iowa Mountaineers	Iowa City
Los Alamos Mountaineers	N. M.
M. I. T. Outing Club	Cambridge, Mass.
Mazamas	Portland, Ore.
Minnesota Rovers	Minneapolis

Mountaineers, Inc.	Seattle
Obsidians	Eugene, Ore.
Olympians, Inc.	Hoquiam, Wash.
Univ. of Oregon Alpine Club	Eugene, Ore.
Pittsburgh Climbers	Penna.
Potomac Appalachian Trail Club	Washington, D. C.
Rensselaer Mountaineering Club	Troy, N. Y.
Rimrock Mountaineers	Coulee Dam, Wash.
Sierra Club	

(Has Rock Climbing Section, Desert Peaks Section, Chapters in San Diego, Los Angeles, PaloAlto-San Jose, Fresno, San Francisco)

Smoky Mountains Hiking Club	Knoxville, Tenn.
Spokane Mountaineers, Inc.	Wash.
Stanford Alpine Club	Calif.
Trails Club of Oregon	Portland
Wasatch Mountain Club	Salt Lake City, Utah
Washington Alpine Club	Seattle
Wy'east Climbers	Portland, Ore.
Wisconsin Hoofer Mountaineers	Madison
Univ. of Wyoming Outing Club	Laramie
Wyoming Mountaineers	Casper
Yale Mountaineering Club	New Haven

Guide books for some areas have been published, among which those named below will give assistance in becoming familiar with mountains and ranges, but they are not intended for the guidance of novice or inexperienced mountaineers.

Appalachian Mountain Club Katahdin Guide

Appalachian Mountain Club White Mountain Guide

Appalachian Trail Guides

Climber's Guide to the Cascade and Olympic Mountains of the State of Washington — Fred Beckey

Climber's Guide to the High Sierra

Climber's Guide to the Interior Ranges of British Columbia — J. Monroe Thorington

Climber's Guide to the Rocky Mountains of Canada — J. Monroe Thorington

Climber's Guide to the Tetons — Leigh Ortenburgh

Guide to the Colorado Mountains — Robert Ormes

Guide des Alpes Valaisannes — Swiss Alpine Club

Guide Vallot — Groupe de Haute Montagne

Long's Peak, Its Story and a Guide to Climb It — Paul Nesbit
Wanderbuch (walking in Switzerland, a series of regional guides)
Walking In the Alps — J. Hubert Walker

Periodicals of particular interest are published by some of the more prominent mountaineering clubs. In the United States, two of great value are the American Alpine Club's annual *American Alpine Journal* and the Appalachian Mountain Club's semi-annual *Appalachia*. Abroad, the journals of the Alpine Club in London, of the Groupe de Haute Montagne in France, and "Les Alpes" of the Swiss Alpine Club, will prove of service and value.

The lists of clubs, books and periodicals mentioned are in no way exhaustive, nor are they intended to be. They are meant rather to serve as guideposts or cairns, marking the way to the heights. The initial prospect, the route finding, the final attainment are all part of the personal experience that creates the joys of mountaineering.

chapter 15

Good Climbing!

Thou wear'st upon thy forehead clear
The freedom of a mountaineer.
WILLIAM WORDSWORTH

BIG MOUNTAINS make big demands. Whether in effort, technic, judgment or temperament, the climber must be their match. If not, he must confine himself to gazing fondly from the valley. Nothing is more dangerous than carelessness; carelessness derives from fatigue; nowhere does fatigue more readily set in than on an ascent beyond the climber's ability. And exhaustion will always win the day.

Hours of stiff rock climbing are tiring, and so are long snow grinds, twelve hours afoot, lack of sufficient oxygen, expending more effort than required of the situation, cold, wind, irritability. The odds are on the side of the mountain, so in preparing to meet the mountain's demands, it is only common sense to make ready in all phases of the sport, to dress and feed adequately, to refine technics, to allow time for acclimatization, to choose good weather, then to go to the task with the energy and enthusiasm that first brought you to the hills. Thus will the glacier grind become a pleasure, the snow slope and ridge an exhilaration, the summit and descent a source of deep satisfaction.

In whatsoever walk of life, companionship is a prize beyond purchase. Nowhere is friendship and camaraderie more valuable than in the mountains. It is not coincidental that climbers who are en rapport are equal together to greater occasions than either can achieve with others. The famous friendships that were struck between Swiss guides and their "herren" in the early days had much to do with the success of these teams in the opening of the Alps.

In a sense, of course, climbing is a lonely sport, the only actors being the man and the mountain, but because men must climb together as a team, something more than mere sociability creeps in. A common endeavor is shared, often an endeavor of difficulty and sometimes of danger, but thus is a common goal achieved. Both gain the common objective because of the other, yet each by dint of his own efforts.

Possibly in your early climbing years you will meet another mountaineer with whom your style and temperament blend. If common climbing efforts are afforded you, make the most of them, for a friendship may be formed that will be useful to each of you in your years in the high hills. Climb with others, of course, as opportunity offers, for there is much to be learned from the styles and technics of every climber with whom you associate.

There is space in the mountains for the open mind and the open heart. Mountaineers, despite occasional surface gruffness, are people of good will and do their best to keep the world of the mountains a democracy. Quick to frown on any show of false courage, they are equally quick to applaud the well done. In the high places of this world, there is no place for sham.

So take frankness, humility and goodwill with you when you go to the mountains. More is not likely to be asked.

And — good climbing!

Almost there!

Glossary

AVALANCHE. A downpouring of rock, ice or snow.

BELAYING. Protecting a climber by passing the rope around oneself, or around a projection, and paying it out or taking it in as required.

BERGSCHRUND. A crevasse that separates the glacier from the upper slopes of the mountain.

BIVOUAC. A short encampment, usually involuntary.

BUSHWHACKING. Leaving the marked trail and proceeding through the brush or across open country.

CAIRN. A man-made pile of stones for marking the route. Used most frequently above timber-line.

CARABINER. An oval or pear-shaped metal snaplink for placing in the eye of a piton so that the rope may in turn be passed through the carabiner for a climber's protection.

CHIMNEY. A crack or opening sufficiently large for a climber to wedge in or stem across.

COL. A pass between peaks.

CORNICE. A wave-like crest of snow on a ridge.

CRACK. A narrow fissure in rock or ice in which hands or feet may be wedged for ascent.

CRAMPONS. Pointed steel (or aluminum) frames to fit the sole of the climbing boot for use in ascending hard snow or ice.

CREVASSE. Cracks in a glacier caused by the glacier's movement. According to location, crevasses are transverse, longitudinal or marginal.

FACE. Side of a mountain, or a smooth open cliff.

GLACIER. A river of ice.

GLISSADE. To slide down a snow slope, preferably on the feet, occasionally in a *sitz*-position.

GULLY. A wide vertical ravine on a cliff or mountain.

ICE-AX. A climbing implement with adze, point and shaft for use in chopping steps in ice or snow, or as a "third leg" in delicate passages.

ICEFALL. That point on a glacier where descent of the glacier's bed causes the ice to crack and break up.

LAYBACK. A technic of ascent by pulling back with the hands against the opposed pressure and friction of the feet.

MORAINE. The heaped accumulated debris at the sides and foot of a glacier.

OVERHANG. A roof of rock or ice that reaches out over the route.

PITCH. A stretch of rock or snow, usually of some technical difficulty, and frequently not longer than a rope's length.

PITON. A horizontal, vertical or angle-shaped piece of steel with an eye or ring in the end. To be hammered into a crack for use with a carabiner. Round and tubular pitons are used in snow and ice, being pounded in and permitted to freeze in place.

RAPPELLING. Roping down. A method of lowering oneself by passing the rope around the body.

RIDGE. A crest of a mountain with valleys on either side.

RUCKSACK. A knapsack. To be worn on the back by means of shoulder straps.

SCREE. A slope of loose stones and boulders.

SERAC. A tower of ice on a glacier caused by breaking up of the ice from glacier motion. Generally found in an icefall.

SLABS. Smooth sloping rock.

SNOWBRIDGE. Compacted snow reaching across a crevasse or berg-schrund.

Index